Soldiers' Letters Home
A Family's Saga 1863-1919

Other Books by
Eugene Arundel Miller

Railroad 18~~96~~69, Along the Historic Union
    Pacific; ISBN 978-0-9728511-3-8.

A Traveler's Guide to Railroad 1869;
    ISBN 978-0-9728511-4-5.

Photographer of the Early West, The Story of
    Arundel Hull;
    ISBN 978-0-9728511-0-7.

Arundel C. Hull, Ghost Photographer for
    William H. Jackson;
    ISBN 978-0-9728511-1-4.

Soldiers' Letters Home
A Family's Saga 1863-1919

Eugene Arundel Miller

Antelope-Press
410 Monte Vista Ave.
Mill Valley, California 94941-5081

Soldiers' Letters Home
A Family's Saga 1863-1919

By Eugene Arundel Miller

Printed in the United States of America ....Copyright 2011

Publisher's Cataloging-In-Publication Data
(Prepared by The Donohue Group, Inc.)

Miller, Eugene A. (Eugene Arundel)
   Soldiers' letters home: a family's saga, 1863-1919 / Eugene Arundel Miller.

   p. : ill., maps ; cm.

   Includes bibliographical references.
   ISBN: 978-0-9728511-2-1

   1. Soldiers--United States--Correspondence. 2. Spanish-American War, 1898--Personal narratives. 3. United States--History--Civil War, 1861-1865--Personal narratives. 4. World War, 1914-1918--Personal narratives. 5. United States--History, Military. 6. Miller, Eugene A. (Eugene Arundel)--Family. I. Title.

E181 .M55 2011
973/.092   2011905358

Antelope-Press
410 Monte Vista Ave.
Mill Valley, California 94941-5081

Acknowledgements

I especially wish to thank Phyllis, my wife, and Vicki Weiland, editor extraordinaire, for their positive critical commentary, suggestions, and corrections throughout my efforts.

Photographs and Illustrations are credited as noted adjacent to them. Most of the photographs are from various family collections: Arundel Miller Hull, Nina Hull Miller, and Glenn E. Miller.

Several photographs relating to the Spanish-American War are from collections held by the Nebraska State Historical Society whose permission is gratefully acknowledged.

Other photographs are acknowledged where it was possible to determine their origin. They are believed to be in the public domain.

Several original photographs have seriously deteriorated. Although they are of poor quality they have been included where they add substantially to the text.

Maps have been prepared by the author. For those in Parts III and IV the digital assistance of photographer Lois Tema has been crucial. Thanks!

My thanks for the exceptional cover which has been created and refined by Joel Friedlander of Marin Bookworks.

Dedication

This book is dedicated to those hundreds of thousands of young men, women, and families whose lives have been profoundly changed by their experiences in the armed services.

Preface

Among the family keepsakes preserved and passed along to me were collections of letters and photographs from three family members who had served in the armed forces of the United States.

The letters home from Judson Elliot Miller (Civil War), Arundel Miller Hull (Spanish-American War), and Glenn Eugene Miller (World War I) are not startlingly dramatic but they provide a non-glamorized insight of the experiences of three soldiers in three different wars.

All three young men were motivated by patriotism and their desire to explore beyond their locale. Each of the young letter writers tried to reassure their families of their well-being. However, as they witnessed the cruel and grim realities that war brings, their ardor plummets and their views change.

As we research their wars and the pretext for them we gain an insight into how these soldiers were affected. However, in the context of their time, the letters are more meaningful for what they *do not tell*. In this book I attempt to share some insights these letters provide with other family members, descendants, historians, and fellow readers.

Eugene Arundel Miller

Partial Ancestor Tree

Jacob Hull
    m.1821 Clarissa Arundel
	Alanson Miller
	    m.1830 Charlotte Marshall

Eliza Hull
Jacob Hallett Hull
Clarissa Elizabeth Hull
David Dick Hull
Ester Hull
Charles Coventry Hull
William Henry Harrison Hull
George Washington Hull
Arundel C. Hull —— m.1873

Susan Miller Phelps
Cornelia Miller Green
Judson Elliot Miller
Angeline Miller Atkins
Jared Alanson Miller
Charlotte Miller Smith
Florence Cecilia Miller Hull

Arundel Miller Hull
    m. Adelaide Deily

Clyde Charles Hull
    m. Amy Dorothy Weatherby

Florence Clarissa Hull

Bessie Evangeline Hull
    m. Beyer Aune

May Charlotte Hull
    m. Elmer Ellis

Nina Irene Cecilia Hull
    m. 1921 **Glenn Eugene Miller**

Glenn Hull Miller
Millicent Miller Sacio
Eugene Arundel Miller

(Men with **bolded** names sent letters home.)

Contents

List of Maps

"Lady Liberty" circa 1863.

Part I 1863
Judson's Civil War Journey

Judson Elliot Miller

Judson Elliot Miller

Judson was born in Constantia, New York March 28, 1836 to Alanson Miller and Charlotte Marshall Miller. When he was age 10 his family moved westward to a farm near Racine, Wisconsin, then to the Colorado gold country: Central City, Black Hawk, and Gold Dirt. There on October 18 1862, at age 26, he enlisted in the Colorado Volunteer Infantry. Assigned to Company D, 3rd Regiment, he trained at Camp Weld north of Denver then marched across eastern Colorado and Kansas into Missouri. Later the Company became Company L, 2nd Colorado Cavalry and Judson was promoted to Corporal.

He was in Missouri October 2, 1864 when he died of dysentery. Judson was buried at Independence, Missouri alongside his Company captain and six of his fellow soldiers.

1. A Different War

During the 1850s there was great turmoil in the United States with the Southern states' increasing opposition to Northern states' political dominance.

After Lincoln became president, in 1861 seven Southern states seceded from the Union and formed the Confederate States of America.

In Missouri a state convention on secession voted to remain with the Union. The pro-Confederate governor called out the state militia, but Union forces chased the governor and his militia to the southwestern corner of the state. The state convention then reconvened and elected a pro-Union state government.

Radical, anti-slavery abolitionists, primarily from Kansas, staged attacks on pro-slavery partisans in Missouri. The Missourians, in turn, organized guerrilla raiding parties that roamed the state burning crops, farms, and killing partisans without constraint.

The 40,000 guerrilla raiders were so effective that the Union assigned 60,000 troops to Missouri to quell their rampages.[1] However, the inept Union leadership and their increasingly repressive tactics drove hundreds of otherwise neutral Missourians into the guerilla ranks.

Elsewhere across the South the Union's advantages in manpower, industry, finance, and transportation began to overwhelm the Southern forces. In 1865 the Confederacy collapsed with General Lee's surrender at Appomattox. In Missouri, the insurgent raiding parties dwindled as scattered members took advantage of Union offers of amnesty. Others saw they had no chance for a peaceful life and continued their outlaw lives of robbery and murder roaming the West.

---

[1] Brownlee, Richard S., Gray Ghosts of the Confederacy, Guerrilla Warfare in the West 1861-1865.

2. Judson Signs Up

Sometime in 1846 or 1847 the Miller family and several family groups moved from New York to Racine, Wisconsin settling on farms near one another. The Miller family included Alanson's spouse Charlotte Marshall Miller, sons Judson Elliott Miller and younger brother, Jared, and five sisters, Susan, Cornelia, Angeline, Charlotte, and Florence.

Not satisfied with farming several men joined the California Gold Rush, coming back full of enthusiasm about "the West." After several years several families again joined together to move farther west, this time to Central City in the Colorado gold country 35 miles west of Denver.[2] In 1863 and 1864, as the men prospected claims, the families lived in Central City, then in Black Hawk and Gold Dirt.[3] During part of that time the Millers

---

[2] In 1859 gold was discovered 35 miles west of Denver in a gulch near Central City. Within two months the population grew to 10,000 people seeking their fortunes. It was soon the leading mining center in Colorado and became known as "The Richest Square Mile on Earth."

[3] Black Hawk adjoins Central City. The Gold Dirt town site is a few miles from present day Rollinsville, Colorado. Gold Dirt had

ran a trading post and then a store. Later they moved to Denver.

Nina Hull Miller Collection

Central City, Colorado – 1868.

When President Lincoln called for volunteers, Colorado responded with nearly 4,000 men. In the Colorado gold country the tug of patriotism and the disappointment with mining success moved many men to "join up." In Central City Judson Elliott

---

its heyday from 1862 to 1864. With a population of about 500, it boasted an impressive array of log cabins, with stores and saloons along its main street.

Miller, along with numerous others, responded to the call for service, leaving parents and siblings behind.[4]

Judson enlisted in the newly organized Company D, 3rd Infantry Regiment of the Colorado Volunteers. They were trained at Camp Weld just north of Denver. Starting in March 1863 the volunteers marched eastward across eastern Colorado to Kansas, arriving in Fort Leavenworth seven weeks later. After a short stop they continued eastward to St. Louis. By the end of April they had traversed nearly 850 miles.

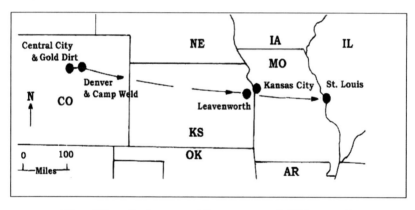

**The March Across Kansas and Missouri.
Judson's Unit Marched 850 Miles to St. Louis.**

In the letters he wrote to his mother, he tells her of his unit's moves to various camps in Missouri, then into Arkansas, up the Missouri

---

[4] Several months after Judson Miller left for war, Jared, his 19-year-old brother, died of mountain fever at Gold Dirt. These two were the only sons in the family and with them ended that Miller-named line of descendants.

River, and back across Missouri. In November 1863 Judson's unit became part of the Company L, 2nd Colorado Cavalry under Captain Galen Norton, and Judson was promoted to Corporal.

His unit was located along the Missouri River east of Kansas City and near Independence where the Union troops engaged in numerous skirmishes with the raiders and insurgent bands.

He often wrote his mother reassuring her about his health and speculating that the War would be over by "next year." Judson never described any of the fighting, but his unit was engaged often in or near some of the heavy battles. In his letters he commented about the devastation left in the wake of the fighting, but never told of fights directly. More than likely he wanted to avoid alarming his mother. It is evident that he was homesick. In response to his mother's constantly asking when he would come home Judson kept reassuring her that he was alright. In one of his letters he told his mother that he thought he better find a wife when he got out of the service.

Judson's service mirrored many other individuals of the day. They were patriots and anxious to do their part for their country, knowing not what the future held. Many of them, perhaps most, would not return.

The soldiers killed in actual battlefield fighting and those claimed by mortal wounds numbered in the thousands.

Like many others however, Judson died, not of wounds, but of dysentery, which took more lives in the Civil War than bullets. He was 28 years old. Each of those soldier's lives is a poignant story of its own. Judson's military service was not a hero's tale but his death from dysentery put his military life into the book of "Ordinary Heroes" of whom there were thousands.

In a letter notifying Judson's family of his death Captain Norton wrote, *"He was sick less than three days. We did not look for him to die until it was too late to talk to him in relation to his family … Judson was beloved by all the company officers and men … burial was in Independence Cemetery by the side of eight men who were killed with Capt Waggoner."* The letter was signed by Galen G. Norton, Capt. Co. L, 2nd Colorado Cavalry.

Judson's handwritten letters were initially transcribed by his niece Nina Hull Miller. She commented, "He usually neglected to begin sentences with a capital letter and omitted periods at the end. However, after he began corresponding with George Nobles, who had been his teacher in Wisconsin and who wrote perfect letters, Judson began using periods and sometimes capitals."

The transcriptions included here have been partially edited by adding punctuation and making minor changes for clarity. Portions of the text which seem extraneous have been omitted. The omissions are indicated by ellipses.

Sample of Judson's Handwriting.

3. First Letters Home, 1863

Judson's first letter home was written soon after his arrival at Leavenworth, Kansas. There the Colorado Volunteers had a brief rest stop before continuing their march to St. Louis then south into Confederate territory.

Camp Leavenworth   Sunday April 26, 1863

Dear Mother and Father and the rest.

I am well and happy and hope this will find you the same. We got in here last Thursday, 23rd. We had a pleasant time, no storms. Only a few sick and only one death and he died by the effects of the cursed whiskey.

Mother you cannot guess who I found here, well it was T. P. Marshall. He has got a daguerreotype. He took a picture of me which I will send to you.

We are camped on a nice little green knoll as smooth as can be. [It is] 2 miles from the City, Leavenworth [and] is quite a place. The Fort is the pirties [prettiest] place. All the houses is [are] painted white. U. S. has a nice farm here some 2 miles square. I expect we will go to St. Louis this week. ... And from there we know not.

Charlotte, you and Florence write me will you and Jared too.[5] I wish you all would....

It is all quiet here. They call the Rebels the Copperheads.[6] There is only a few companies stopped at the Fort now. They are all the time going and comin. .... My love to all Mother, from your boy.

Judson E. Miller[7]

---

[5] Charlotte, Florence, and Jared are Judson's siblings.
[6] A Copperhead was more commonly used for Northerners who opposed the Civil War and sometimes sabotaged the war effort.
[7] Judson signed his letters with several variations of his name.

Judson's Travels During 1863.

Bloomfield, Mo.   *Jul 15th 1863*

Dear Mother,

I received yours of the 21st last today and you better believe I was glad to hear you are all well and hardy as can be. We left Pilot Knob the first of July and here we are some 75 miles from Pilot Knob. I thought that we should stay there all summer but General Davidson detailed our company to go with the Pontoon bridge. The rest of the Reg't is [not] up to Pilot Knob yet. You know what a pontoon bridge is, don't you? You have seen them in the pictures. They are a curious thing. I cannot describe them very well.[8]

...We cannot tell how long we shall stay here. I am in an old house close to camp. It is a good place to write, [and] there is an old writing desk there to write on....

This is a rather dull place. Nearly all the houses vacant. Nearly all the people were Sesesh [Secessionists]. They had a fight here a year ago and all the Rebels got up and left.

---

[8] A pontoon bridge is a temporary bridge whose deck is supported on a series of flat bottomed floats or boats.

Nina Hull Miller Collection

Pontoon Boats in Transit to a Bridge Site.

Nina Hull Miller Collection

Pontoon Bridge with Plank Roadway.
(example)

There are a few [Rebels] here yet but they perfess [profess] to be loyal. There are some fifteen thousand troops of ours here. We have had a great deal of rain and very muddy roads. We had the bridge down once and that was on the Mingo Swamp 20 miles from here....

Mother, do not worry any more about me for I will take good care of my health. We have good doctors ... I think the war will close before next summer.

Tell Elix[9] I wish he would write and tell me all about Gold Dirt and Leads.

I cannot think of anything more to write so good bye from your affectionate boy.
Judson E. Miller.
Direct yours to
Co. D Pontoon Battalion Arma, S. E. Mo.

---

[9] "Elix" is a nickname for Alex Atkins, Judson's brother-in-law.

Mingo Swamp

Bloomfield and the nearby Mingo Swamp are in the southeast corner of Missouri. Earlier in 1863, the Union's Missouri Militia surprised a troop of Confederate partisans at Simon Cato's farm in the Mingo Swamp. The Militia killed nine and fatally wounded twenty of the partisans. Cato, a 64-year-old farmer, was said to be harboring "outlaws" and was killed. News of the event, called the "Mingo Massacre," spread rapidly among the Confederates and helped trigger brutal retaliation.

Pilot Knob Friday,   August the 21st 1863

Dear Mother and the rest of you,

Forgive me for not writing sooner. We got back a week ago the 14th. ... We had a very good time down south in Rakensack[10], we called it. I will give you the detail of our march as near as I can. We left there the next day,

---

[10] Rackensack is the Osage Indian name for the mountainous Ozark Plateau between the Arkansas and Missouri Rivers.

traveled 10 [days] to St. Luke, [Louis] stayed one day. We camped in a nice peach orchard and there was a nice spring. We left there the 19th and camped 2 miles off the St. Francis [River]. In the morning we got down to the river. We helped lay down the bridge in the for[fore] noon and in the afternoon we crossed the river and camped on Chalk Bluffs the 20th. We have 12 buternut[11] prisoners to guard. We stay here today. Poor country around here. There was some Rebels here... The advance guard units made them run. They did not catch any....

We are in Arkansas, traveled 10 [miles] today. We camped in Seaterville and the boys found lots of things the Rebels hid. ... We found sugar, salt meat, shot dried peaches, cap and a pair of socks. We had a big mess of chickens.

---

[11] Butternut referred to Confederate soldiers who wore uniforms of homespun cloth dyed with a mixture of walnuts and copper which produced a brown-yellowish (butternut) hue.

One of the boys found lots of dried tobacco. None but women left. The men all leave when they hear we are coming....

We camped near Gainesville. The boys found some letters written by the women to their husbands and lovers. They think the Yankees are reckless savages. We camped at Greens Bourge. Now these little towns is deserted. One of our boys got arrested for trying to open a safe. He is in the guard house now.

We did not start from camp until afternoon. We camped near a grist mill. The men ran and left the mill arunin when they heard we were coming. When we got there some of the soldiers were running the mill.

We are all [the] infantry there is with the brigade. The rest of them are cavalry and artillery. There are twelve thousand in the brigade commanded by General Davidson, an old Rebel?

We camped near some Rebel women's houses, 28th. We got into Wittsburg today. It is on the St Francis. We camped on a high hill with a small battery. The boats come up the river as far as here.

This has been a business place before the War. This is cotton country. I have seen cotton and cane, the tobacco too. We laid here until the first of August then started for Helena. Got there the 5th and was ordered back here to our regiment. We passed some good country. We had all the peaches we wanted. We passed lots of nice fields all grown up to weeds. We stayed in Helena 2 days and started for St Genevieve.

We were the only company that came up on the boat. We had a good time the 2 days coming up on the boat. We stopped at Memphis to change boats and that is a very fine place. We passed Cairo Island No. 10 and several other places. We got off the boat at eleven o'clock at night at St. Genevieve the 11th. We got here the 14th. We had plenty, 45 miles, from St. Genevieve to here. I expect we will stay here some time.

Union Gunboats Patrolled the Rivers.

Oh I almost forgot ... my bunkie Philips was left down at Bloomfield sick ...Oh how I would like to see you all. ... I cannot tell how soon I will come but I will come as soon as I can. Perhaps by the time this reaches you Pa and Carve[12] will be back. Give my respects to all my inquiring friends. Jared,[13] if Pa comes tell him to dun Wagner the recruiting officer for 2 dollars that he borrowed from me in Denver. If he can get it you may have it. I have some sixty dollars with me. If it would go safely I would send it home but I am afraid it would not. ... Dear ones good bye. Mother farewell, write soon. From your affectionate boy,

Judson E. Miller,

Co. D, 3rd Regt, Col Vols. Pilot Knob, Mo.

---

[12] Sister Cornelia's husband Carver Green.
[13] Jared was Judson's young brother.

Chasing Marmaduke

In April 1863, when Judson's outfit was in Leavenworth, Rebel General Marmaduke had gathered 5,000 men in Arkansas and advanced northward into Missouri to strike the Union Army at Bloomfield. Twelve hundred of his new recruits were without weapons but he ordered them northward anyway because he feared if he left them behind they would desert.

Marmaduke's Army bogged down in the spring mud and superior Union forces moved in to repel them. The Southerners retreated from Bloomfield to a crossing of the St. Francis River at Chalk Bluff, where they feverishly built a crude foot bridge for the retreating soldiers. After nightfall Marmaduke's men crossed single file and then dragged their artillery pieces across on hastily lashed together log rafts. Their horses were forced to swim across and many of them did not make it in the swift water. Before dawn the bridge was cut loose to float downstream.

In the early light of the following day 250 more Confederate troops arrived at the crossing. With the Union troops in pursuit, the troopers swam across with their horses to the Arkansas shore. The Union artillery peppered the Confederates still in the valley bottom and in turn received volleys from the Rebels firing from the top of the Chalk Bluffs along the opposite bank. The exchange of artillery and small arms fire continued for hours. The Confederates stalemated and retreated, slogging through the swampy low ground along the river.

One Confederate Colonel wrote:[14]

"Day after day, in mud and water, with artillery, baggage, and ammunition wagons mired down, and horses and mules floundering in exhaustion, did my men toil and struggle, when after three days of untold trials and hardships, the entire command emerged from this wilderness of mud and disease-generating miasma more like an army of denizens of a semi-amphibious subterranean world than one of men and animals."

---

[14] "Rugged and Sublime: The Civil War in Arkansas," Department of Arkansas Heritage.

The Union forces reported their casualties at Chalk Bluff as 23 killed, 44 wounded, and 53 captured. Marmaduke's Confederate forces had greater casualties due in part to the addition of 150 raw untrained recruits rounded up from nearby counties just before the encounter.

National Archives and Records, Civil War Photos

A Short Rest for Weary Soldiers in Missouri.

The Union forces did not immediately pursue the Rebels but soon followed them. Within a month Judson's outfit left their camps at Pilot Knob and moved southward on the high ground along the west side of the St. Francis River. As he mentioned in his previous letter home, he was in a detachment tasked to put a pontoon bridge across the river. Afterward they were sent farther south to Helena, some 120 miles into Arkansas.

Harper's Pictorial History

Union Camp at Pilot Knob.

Drawing From Judson's Letterhead
"FRONT FACE !!"
**"Why in the thunder don't you cast your eyes
to the front!!"**

Pilot Knob,   Sunday Sept. 20th, 1863
Dearest Mother,
        I will write you a few lines to let you know
that I have not forgotten you nor the rest of you
(excuse this pirty [pretty] picture) [meaning
the letterhead] I have not had a letter from you
since we were in Bloomfield the 14th of July. ... I
expect the letters got miscarried. I am well now
but have not been for two or three weeks back.

We have a good doctor and we do not have many sick. It is a healthy place here.

I received a letter from Dear Angie[15] and Jim the 25th of August. I answered them a week after. Oh was I glad to get one from Dear Angie, you bet I was. I read it over and over but not as often as I do yours Dear Mother. I received one from Jo and Dear Neel[16] the same day we got in from Arkansas.

Dear Mother, ...I have been enlisted just 11 months yesterday, almost a year. I have not yet been in a battle yet and I do not think we will be. I think the war will be over before long and I will skedaddle for home. But I must stay until the War is over... maybe two years longer. I would like to see you all. Happy would I be to come in now and surprise you all, but I must wait until my time is out.

---

[15] Judson's sister Angeline Miller Atkins.
[16] Judson's sister Cornelia Miller Green.

Only think Dear Mother what sighs of mothers that have sons and husbands in the Army. You little know what suffering this cursed war makes.

Lots of Union people coming in here every day to get away from the Rebels. Some have been robbed of everything, some just escaped with their lives. Some of the women have seen their husbands shot down right before their eyes by the merciless hellhounds. This state is full of Bushwhackers and Copperheads. I hope they will be wiped out so there will not be a Rebel left to live by next summer

We have two brothers the name is Root, in our company, that had their folks in Lawrence. They were burned out and robbed of all they had and just escaped with their lives. You have heard about the Quantrill's Massacree [Massacre] in

Lawrence. Phillips[17] knew lots of the people who were killed.

I have seen where the Arkansas Traveler[18] stayed all night. I will have lots of stories to tell you when I get home. I expect by the time this gets there Father will be home. If so tell Pa to write about the new Mines. I cannot think of anything more to write at this time. My love to all. Sharl and Flum,[19] you both may comb my hair, it itches now. Good by Dearest Mother from your affectionate boy,
J. E. Miller

---

[17] A fellow soldier.
[18] William Quantrill, leader of a guerilla band.
[19] Judson's sisters Charlotte and Florence.

The Sack of Lawrence

William Quantrill led one of the several pro-Confederate guerilla bands. They roamed Missouri and carried out numerous raids, sacking and killing without constraint.

In August 1863, only a few weeks after Judson's outfit passed through Fort Leavenworth, Quantrill's guerrillas swept into Lawrence, Kansas. There, for four hours, 400 mounted raiders systematically burned all commercial buildings and all but one house. Following Quantrill's orders "not a man in Lawrence was to be alive when they got off their horses," they left 150 dead.

The sack of Lawrence was particularly brutal, but many who lived in the surrounding area were Confederate sympathizers and provided refuge for Quantrill's guerrillas and other bushwhackers.[20]

Within four days of the attack on Lawrence, Union General Ewing issued sweeping General Order No. 11. With certain exceptions, all residents in four Missouri border counties were ordered to leave their homes and clear out of the area.

---

[20] Bushwhackers were loosely organized vandals, usually Confederates, operating in remote rural areas.

GENERAL ORDER No. 11

First:

All persons living in Cass, Jackson, and Bates Counties and in that part of Vernon County are hereby ordered to move from their present places of residence within 15 days.

Those who within that time establish their loyalty to the satisfaction of the commanding officer of the military station nearest their present place of residence will receive from him certificates stating the facts of their loyalty and the names by whom it can be shown. All who receive such certificates will be permitted to remove to any military station in this district or to any part of the state of Kansas, except the counties on the eastern borders of the state.

All others shall remain out of the district.

Second:

All grain or hay in the fields or under shelter in the district ... after the ninth of September will be taken to such stations and turned over to the proper offices there; and report ... made to district headquarters specifying the names of all loyal owners. All grain and hay found in such district after the ninth of September next ... will be destroyed.

Union forces proceeded to burn the buildings and fields in the four border counties leaving a desolate countryside, presumably unable to support the guerillas and Confederate raiders.

Thurs. Oct 1, 1863

Dearest Sister Angie,   *Gold Dirt Colo*

    I received yours to [me] August 3rd today, not ten minutes ago. So you see I am prompt in answering it. You bet I was glad to hear from you and the rest of the folks. I got one too from Quill Davis today too dated August 11th. It seems that these letters have been way down south. We were only gone from here a month and a half. I received [the letter] from you the 25th of August. It found me in the hospital. I answered it a few days after.

    Jimmy Kelsey received one from his Mother the same day as he was in the Hospital the same time. He is well now and sent $25 to his Mother the other day. Tell his folks if you see any of them he is well, steady as an old man. He makes a good Soldier and a good boy and sends his love to all of them.

I am well. Tell Elek that the boys that left Denver last of August, that belong to our Company, got here 3 days ago. The old man Tuttle was one of them, Jack Brimness father-in-law. Jack is the same old Jack of old, tells more stories than you can shake a stick at as Carve says. I suppose Carve can tell some about the new mines. You will have lots to tell me when I get home.

I cannot tell when that will be. I have been in almost a year. It will be on the 19th of this month. I may have to stay in two more years, cannot tell. Tell Mother I wrote her on the 20th of last month, on the 28 too and sent her forty dollars the 25th. I bought a watch and had 32 dollars stolen from me or I should have sent one hundred for her use and take care of.

Capt. G. G. Norton is the best officer we have in the outfit. ... We can pick out four or five officers that need cashiering ... [but]We have three as good as officers as there are in the outfit. I believe I told you all about our march down south in my last letter that was worth mentioning. We had a good time down there. We only went as far as Helena but that is getting well down south....

Give my love to one and all and keep a heap for yourself Dear Sister. Farewell, your affectionate Brother,

Elliot Miller, Co. D. 3rd Regt, Colo. Vol.

Pilot Knob, Mo.   *Oct 6, 1863*

                    In the tent sitting on my bed

Dear Brother, [Jared]

    I received yours of Sept 20ᵗʰ yesterday and was glad to hear from home once more. I am well and hardy now....

    I have sent money Home. It was ten days ago. I was glad to hear Pa and Carve got back and are doing well. I would like to see you all but I am contented as I can be.

    You bet I am going to save all the money I can so when I get out I will have something to start on. When you spoke about Pa selling the team [horses] *did you mean Chub and Charley? If it is, it is alright. ... I hope so....*

    I cannot tell you whether we will stay here all winter or not. We got back from down south August 14 gone from here one month and a half. I will have to wait until I get back to tell you about our trip.

The boys are playing cards to see who will cut the wood for tonight. We have a stove in our tent. I will tell you the names of the boys. First is Philips, my bunkey, Jack Brimener, Bill Hardy, Charley Boot, Burt Crawford, Nell's Cousin Cho, P. Rupee, J. Blair, W. Barns, McKibben. Jimmy Kelsey has gone out.

That is all. Tell Mother not to worry about me. We have a good place here, enough to eat and [clothing to] wear and nothing to do. Jared we have a good time. Philips and me has a bushel of walnuts. We got this afternoon and plenty of them and apples till you can't rest. All we want, cost nothing.

We had some cool weather here. It was raining a little.

Tell me about Elik and Angie and Gold Dirt and Black Hawk . ... Give my respects to inquiring friends, my love to all the folks. Hoping these few lines will find you all well and happy. From your Brother

Ell. Co. D, 3rd Reg. Colo. Vols. Pilot Knob Mo.

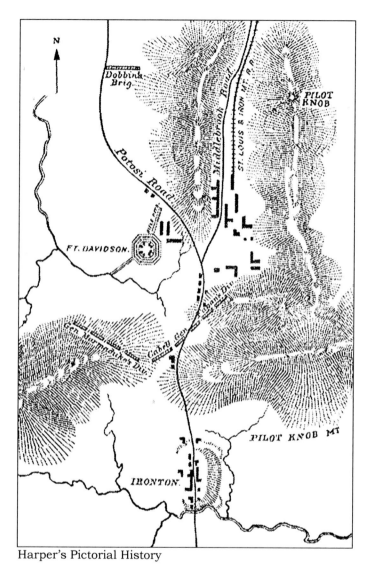

Harper's Pictorial History

Pilot Knob, Fort Davidson, and Ironton.

Battle of Pilot Knob (or Fort Davidson)

About a year after Judson was stationed at Pilot Knob, the Confederates staged a major offensive intent on capturing St. Louis.[21] One of their first objectives was to capture the Union Fort Davidson at Pilot Knob. The town was the terminus of the railroad from St. Louis and was thus important for moving Union troops and supplies.

The fort was defensively strong with ten-foot thick walls nine-feet high. Two long rifle pits extended out from the walls. It was surrounded by a dry moat nine-feet deep and crossed by a single drawbridge. A clear field of fire extended 300 yards out in all directions. The fort was armed with seven pieces of artillery and had a garrison of 1,500 men, more than enough to man the walls. In contrast, the Confederate Army, headed by Major General Sterling Price, and bent on the capture of the fort, was comprised of 12,000 men.

As the Confederate troops advanced on Pilot Knob and nearby Ironton, the Union forces withdrew into the fort. The following day the fort was attacked by Confederate brigades, from all four directions, but not simultaneously. The Union could therefore concentrate their defensive guns on each Confederate brigade as they attacked. As the

---

[21] National Park Service battle description.

Rebel troops got close enough, they were peppered with hand-grenades tossed over the walls and repulsed. Rebuffed for the day, the Confederates fell back into the woods and through the night they concentrated on building scaling ladders.

After a three-day siege the Union troops decided their position was untenable. They draped canvas over the drawbridge to screen it and muffle their sounds, and under darkness escaped the fort and withdrew to the north undetected. As they did so they left a slow burning fuse in the powder magazine. The entire magazine later exploded in a magnificent blast that lit up the surrounding countryside.

Although General Price's troops clamored to pursue the escaping Union soldiers, the General demurred. Over ten percent of the Confederate army had been lost and three days wasted.

The Pilot Knob battle casualties, killed and wounded, have been estimated at 1,000 Confederates and 200 Union troops. Since the Confederates "held the field" they had the burden of burying the dead. One of the rifle pits was selected for a mass grave to hold both Confederate and Union soldiers.

Confederate 13-Star Flag.

Union 33-Star Flag.

Ft. Wyman, Rolla, Mo.,   *Nov. 6, 1863*

C. T. Miller, Simpson House.

Dear Mother,

     We got here from Pilot Knob ten days ago. We have had very stormy weather until three days back. It has been pleasant since, very warm and pleasant today. I am on guard here at Ft. Wyman. We are camped here close to town about a mile from the town of Rolla. We have good times here. I expect you have heard about our Regt being consolidated with the 2nd Regt, Colo. Vols.[22] And we are Cavalry now but have not got our horses yet. Cannot tell when we will get them....

     Dear [sister]*Angie wrote that they were going to move down from Gold Dirt to Denver before long. She told me that Elek had been sick and poor*

---

[22] About this time Judson was promoted to Corporal.

Julie[23] had not got married yet. Oh how my heart aches for the poor Gal but I shall pity the unlucky man that gets her the most. That is if she be fortunate to get one....

This is a very pleasant place in pleasant weather but I do not like Missouri. It is very hilly and rough. This has been covered over with timber but it is all cut off now [and] it is poor soil.

I have not seen a prairie since we came from Ft. Leavenworth and that was in the northern part of the state between St. Joseph and Hannibal.

We have twenty prisoners here in the fort. Some are Rebels, some are hard looking easterners. Capt G. G. Norton is the Officer of the Day. Mrs. Norton was up here today looking at the Fort. They live in town. Jared we [have] four big guns here in the Fort called the Seege [siege] guns. Most big enough to stick ones head in I bet.

---

[23] A neighbor's daughter.

Tell Charlotte and Flum there are some girls about their size peddling apples everyday and they are very bold. The town is full of women refugees from the South come in to keep from starving. Uncle Sam has to feed a great many women. Well Dear Mother, I must bid you good by for this time.

Tell Jared I thank him very much for his long letter he wrote in Denver and Gold Dirt. Hoping my Dear Mother that this finds you all well. I remain your affectionate boy,
Judson E. Miller.
Direct as before only Rolla, Mo.

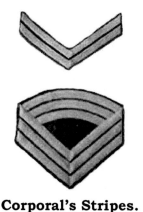

Corporal's Stripes.

Rolla and Fort Wyman

Before the Civil War, Rolla was a town of about 600 civilians and an important freight terminus critical for the movement of Union troops and supplies. Thousands of Union troops arrived there by train, formed up with their supply trains, and advanced south to meet the Confederate forces in southern Missouri and northern Arkansas.

In 1861, when the Union Army was defeated at Wilson's Creek, they fell back to Rolla. There, in defense of the town, the troops threw up a 400-foot-square earthen fort, Fort Wyman. The outer walls were sheathed with slanted timbers to deter climbers. The fort was entirely surrounded by a dry moat and armed with 32-pound artillery pieces. Within a mile radius of town the troops dug a series of other earthworks and trenches as outer defenses.

In 1863, Fort Dette was added to the town's defenses. It was built in a cross shape and was equipped with 24-pound pieces. Over 20,000 troops were garrisoned in the town and at the two forts.

Ft Wyman, Mo. [Rolla]   Nov, 22, 1863

Dear Mother,

Yours of Oct 30th and Nov 8th came to hand yesterday and you better believe I was glad but very sorry to hear that you were sick. It found me well. Received a letter from you and one from Angie some two weeks ago. ...She said they talked of moving from Gold Dirt. She said she would write so I would know where to direct it.

You can't guess who I found here, a Sogering from Wisconsin. I have been to see him four times and took four meals with him. They are in the 2nd Wis. Cav. Regt Co. G. It [the company] was raised in Racine County. The company is acting as Provost Guard in the town. Well dear Mother I am not there to hear you guess so I will have to tell you, well one is George W. Nobles[24], Ed Carr, Bill Butler and I

---

[24] George Nobles had been Judson's teacher in Racine.

first saw him in the guard house. He is in there. I came off guard this morning. Here comes the dinner. I will have to stop a spell to eat it. Here goes. We had some beans, beef, bread, coffee, sugar. That is all good enough....

Dear Mother you will see the time when you will see me a comin Home and free from bad habits as I was when I left Home, but many a mother will find her boy different than he was when he left Home. Some has learned to drink gamble sware and use tobacco and some that did not drink gets drunk now. The Army is a hard place for boys....

They had another Draft in Racine Co. 504 drafted there. Oscar Nobles, George Green, Gust Numann and that was all I knew of the drafted. George Nobles had a list of the names of the drafted men. George thinks the boys will pay the three hundred dollars first before they will go.[25] I wish it

---

[25] Men who could afford it could pay someone else to serve in the army in their place.

had been Jim instead of George so he could get away from his old Dad. The dam Copperhead. George says there are a good many Copperheads around Skunk Grove[26]....

You were saying something about whether I had seen a pirty [pretty] girl or not. No, not here in Missouri nor since I left home. They are the homblest [homeliest] set of women in Missouri I ever saw. ...I have not seen as good looking girls as Sharl and Flum is.

We have not got our horses yet. I think we will not get them until spring. Tell Father the Capt of Georges Co. G is Lawyer Dake of Racine.

Hoping this finds you all well. I bid you good by Dear Mother and the rest of you. From your affectionate son,

Judson E. Miller.

Co D, 3rd Reg. Colo. Vols. Rolla, Mo.

---

[26] Skunk Grove, now named Franksville, is a village about five miles west of Racine, Wisconsin, Judson's former home town.

**Judson's Letter
Mailed from Benton Barracks.**

Benton Barracks was built in 1861, about four miles west of the present day city of St. Louis. It was an enormous temporary billets where troops were mustered into service and new army units organized. With mile long rows of barracks and warehouses, cavalry stables, a large military hospital, a prison and parolee encampment, the barracks could accommodate 30,000 soldiers.

Judson's outfit was moved to Benton Barracks for conversion into a cavalry company.

Benton Barracks, St. Louis,

December 10, 1863

Dear Mother,

I take my pen in hand to let you know I am in St. Louis. We got here yesterday from Rolla....

We have got good quarters here. A big room to sleep in. Good bunks and a big kitchen with a big stove with 14 holes in it. The cooks can cook until they can't rest. Four of the boys cook. It is a nice place here for Troops. The barracks here is large enough to accommodate fifteen thousand troops, and the stables enough for as many horses.

Our horses have not come yet but we expect them before long. We expect the rest of the 2rd soon.

I wrote to you Mother about finding George W. Nobles, he is with 2rd Wisconsin Cavalry ...It seems good to see George Nobles and talk over old times with him. I stayed with him the other night. He is going to let me have his picture. When I get it I will send it to you and get mine taken... Here is the apple girl. I must get some to eat. I got four big ones for 5 cents. I wish I could send them to you but cannot, so will eat them myself. George sends his best respects to you all.

I have not told you about the females in Rolla. Well, they smoke, chew tobacco, and sware. They don't think anything of it. Only think Mother how they look with a cud of tobacco in their pirty [pretty] mouths. It is not very small. It is like their feet, large. I will tell you more about them when I get home ....

Phillips has not got back yet from home. He went to New York on a furlow [furlough]. I will send his Ambretype [Ambrotype] to you Mother for you to keep for me, I will get mine taken with my Cavalry Jacket on, and send one to Carv and one to from them....

Tell Sharl and Flum to write a few lines to me. Flum you must learn to dance so when I get home you can dance with me. Excuse the writing Dear Mother. Good by Dear Mother from your affectionate boy,
Judson E. Miller.

Trooper's Slouch Hat.

Unknown artist

**Artist's View of a Typical
Union Soldier.**

4. Last Letters Home, 1864

Judson's Travels, 1864.

In camp near Dresden, Mo.   Jan 28th 1864

Dear Mother.

Yours of the 10th came to hand this morning but it makes me feel sad to think of the sad news it had for me. It don't seem to me poor Jared is dead and that we will never see him again. I feel too sad to write but I will write you a little. [27]

I expected to go to Kansas City right from St. Louis but we are here waiting for orders from our Colonel. He has gone up with four companies. We have been here two weeks, some one hundred and twenty five miles from St. Louis at the end of the Pasiffick [Pacific] Railroad as far as it is finished from Kansas City to St. Louis.

I received a letter from Dear Sister Angie ten days ago. ... I was areading it over last night and it made me feel happy but how different I felt

---

[27] Jared, Judson's younger brother, died December 17, of "mountain fever," a virus infection spread by tick bites.

Dear Mother after reading yours this morning to learn that poor Jared has gone from us forever in this world. Dear Mother, grieve not for he is out of his pain and misery....

I cannot tell you how long we will be here. ... It is a pleasant camp. I have nothing to do but tend my Horse and ride when I want to out to the nabours [neighbors] occasionally, to get dinner, tho the Missourians can't cook like you do Mother. I am well and hope this will find you the same....

I must bid you all good by. My love to all
J. E. Miller,
Co L, 2rd Reg. Colo. Cav. Sedalia Mo.

Union troops had continuing troubles along the western border of Missouri. Despite the oppressive General Order No. 11 many of the occupants remained Southern sympathizers. Although they were not part of the organized Confederate Army, many of them were skilled and resourceful, eager to fight for the South. Without sufficient Union cavalry to police the hamlets and back roads, the sympathizers took cover in their homes and worked secretly with the guerillas and bushwhackers.

Judson's Company was among those troops assigned to pacify the troublesome border counties. They spent the early months of 1864 moving between the towns of Dresden, Sedalia, Johnstown, Harrisonville, Pleasant Hill, and Independence.

Camp Smith, Dresden, Mo. Tuesday Feb 2nd, 1864

Alanson Miller, Golden City [Colo.]
Dear Father,

Yours and Mothers sad but welcome letters came to hand this morning written Dec 25th ....

We have been camped here nearly three weeks. I cannot tell how much longer we will stay here. Four Company has gone with the Colonel to Kansas City. We have had very pleasant weather till within a few days back. It is very muddy here now. The Captains and other officers are attending a Courts Martial.

I think we will go to Kansas City in the course of a week or two. I have an easy a time as one could wish for in the service. I have my Horse to take care of, and stand guard once a week and when I get tired of staying in camp I go out in the Country and get my dinner with the Missourians. Some of them is as great a set of people I ever saw. This is pirty [pretty] country here and it is bound to be wrich [rich] country if it was settled up with enterprising Farmers. It is writch [rich] prairie and well timbered and watered. The Paciffic [Pacific] R. R. is finished as far as here.

I wish you could get a good farm in some good place where there is good nabors [neighbors] so poor Sharl and Flum could go to school and Dear Mother would not have to work anymore. Dear Mother had had to work like a slave and what has she got for it, nothing. Do sell out and let Mother and Sharl and Flum go and stay with Dear Neal and you go into some business that you will not have to work so hard. I think Mother has worked enough....

Yes Father I calculate to return free from bad habits as I left home. Never will I forget the Good Principles that Dear Mother instilled in my mind when I was young. Many is the boy that went into the Army free from bad habits but will return with all the bad habits that a man can have....

Do not let Dear Mother grieve herself to death nor let her work any more. Oh how I wish I could see you all. Kiss Dear Mother for me and Dear Charlotte and Florence to. You must excuse this poor letter. Give my love to all the Dear Folks, my respects to all my Friends. I must Haly [halt] and bid you good by, hoping this will find you all well. I close from your Son,

J. E. Miller,

Co L. 2nd Col Cav, Dresdon, Mo.

In Harrisonville. Mo.   Feb 22. 1864

Dear Mother,

    We have been here for a week today. We had a nice trip from Dresdon, three days on the road. We passed through some nice country, but Mother it looks hard to see such nice farms laid to waste by fire. Some by prairie fire, some set afire and some by Rebels, some by Union men in the first start.

    At first the Rebels was the strongest party here and the Union people had to leave, the ones that could. Some men were shot down, others would have been if the dam Rebels found them. I have seen lots of families that had to leave everything but what they wore. Lots of men had to leave their families to save themselves.

    But when the Union troops came the dam Rebels had to take it, you bet. But there were lots of Rebel men and families that are in the town fed and clothed by Uncle Sam. There are some nice people here but some dam mean ones you bet.

I think we will stay here some time. We have a good time here. We live in brick houses that were used as stores. This had been a nice little town before the War broke out but how it is demolished now.

Dear Mother, little can you guess how much misery this cussed War has made ....

Lew Wait was here yesterday. ... His Company is at Kansas City. He came down to escort a provision train with some others. He is the same old Lew. He told me to tell you he was as ragged and sassy as ever. It seemed good to see him. ...Jim Keem is the only Gold Dirt man that we have here that I know. There are some more in the company with us but I do not know them by name.

We are having pleasant weather here now. Mother I received a letter from George Nobles a while back. I will send it to you so you can see what good letters he writes me... From you affectionate son,

Ell[28]

Direct yours to Co L, 2nd Reg, Col Cav, Harrisonville, Mo.

The Price of Union Disloyalty

At the beginning of the Civil War there were many small communities scattered along the Missouri River. Harrisonville was typical with a population of about 700. Most of them were secessionists and many provided refuge for bushwhackers and other raiders who attacked pro-Union towns in Kansas Territory.

After the sack of Lawrence, in which the entire Kansas town was torched and nearly 200 men were ruthlessly killed, Union General Thomas Ewing issued the infamous General Order No.11. As a result the

---

[28] Judson only occasionally used his middle name, Elliot, or its abbreviation, Ell.

four and a half county area along the western edge of Missouri was cleared of all inhabitants.

Much of the former occupants' hay and grain was subsequently moved to the military stations to augment the Union supplies, where it would be accounted for. All the remaining hay and grain was destroyed and the farms and fields torched, thus rendering the former farmers virtually penniless.

Judson's outfit was camped in the cleared area, at Johnstown, Harrisonville, Pleasant Hill, and Independence. There Judson observed the effects of the drastic General Order No. 11 firsthand and occasionally was part of the Union's subsequent skirmishes with the Confederate raiders.

Harrisonville, Mo.,   Sunday Feb 28th, 1864

Dear Mother,

Yours of the 7th came to hand last Monday. I was happy to hear from you Dear Mother.

This is a good place to Soldier in. We are living in good quarters. Our Co. occupies a whole brick block on the west side of the square. We board out now or have our rations cooked by a woman. We give her thirty cents a week apiece. There are six of us boarding at one place. Most of the Co. is boarding out at different places. Judy is the name of the people where we are boarding. Tell Sharl and Flum there are two girls there but not as dear good girls as you are Dear Sisters. They are clever people. Mr. Judy had to leave his family and farm to save his life from Bushwhackers.

Dear Mother, little can you tell how these Missouri people has had to suffer. Mr. Judy has had two sons shot down in cold blood by the Dam Rebels. Oh how I would like to have it in my power I would send them to hell double quick. The day will come when they will meet their just reward or dues.

There are some families here that have had everything taken from them and their farms destroyed by fire. The country looks desolate after being destroyed by fire. ... The Capt just told me we have marching orders to go some thirty miles from here to a little town called Jonstown. [Johnstown] I cannot tell until after Dress Parade tonight. I will leave this open until after I learn but direct your letters here until you receive one from there, if we go there that is.... My love to all, your affectionate son, Ell.

J. E. Miller

Co L, 2nd Col Cav. Harrisonville, Cass, Co. Mo.

For weeks Quantrill's Confederate raiding party had disappeared into Kansas. In the spring of 1864 when they were spotted working their way up the western edge of Missouri, the civilians and military both reacted in panic. All Union posts were placed on continuous alert and frenzied pleas for troop reinforcement went out to headquarters. Every Kansas town felt as though it were marked for obliteration. "Only the tough young men of the Second Colorado Cavalry found the situation pleasing," The *Kansas City Journal* told its readers. "The Colorado boys were asking for a chance at Quantrill."

Jonstown, [Johnstown] Mo.

Saturday March 12th 1864

Dear Mother,

I take this opportunity to write a few lines.
We are here in a little place called
Jonstown. [Johnstown] It has been a nice place but
far from it now. There are some twenty houses but
more but has been nearly destroyed, tore down and
carried away by Soldiers and Dutch to a place called
Germantown four miles from here where there is one
company of Malatia [militia] stopping. This is rich
and pirty [pretty] country but it looks baron
[barren] and desolate now. I went out with some of
the boys after hay today some six miles from here
and we only saw one house that anyone lives in. We
saw lots of nice farms destroyed by fire, some all
grown up to weeds.

It looked sad to think of the misery and suffering this cussed War has caused. But it is going to be a blessing to Mo. as a state, for it is agoing to free it from the black curse, and that is slavery. It is bound to be free and then people will not be afraid to come here from the North and settle and I do think this is a good farming country down here. But those dam lazy and ignorant Missourians will never make the country look worth anything. If they get plenty of hog and ham money they are contented. This is a good fruit country but they have only the common fruit, hardly any grafted fruit. Let lots of industrious Northerners come and they would make a far different looking country of it....

We have been here some ten days. How long we will stay I cannot tell, maybe all summer. We have a good time here. There are three families moved. A woman and her two, no three girls cook our mess. It tasted better than ... when we cook.

It has been a little over a year Dear Mother since we left Denver. Mac Norton is here. Buckskin we called him, you recollect him do you not. His Company is south of here about 18 miles. Capt Waggoner is his Captain. You recollect Waggoner the man who brought me the wine when I was in the Tent with the Mountain Fever. [back at Gold Dirt, Colorado]

The boys got in with the mail but no letter for me. It takes two men two days to get the mail. Our boys go up some 15 miles to where Co. M is stationed and their boys bring it from Harrisonville to their camp and our boys bring it here....

My love to all from your affectionate boy.

Ell, Co L 2nd Col. Cav. Jonstown, Mo.

Jo[h]nstown Mo.   May 11[th], 1864

Dear Mother,

    I received your much welcome letter of the
14[th] of April 2 days ago. ... It has been very wet
weather here for the last ten days back. We are
here in the old camp yet and a good time we have is a
chiateing [chasing] Bushwhackers. The boys got one
last night. He will be shot today I think ....

    I received the letter that you and Carve wrote
some ten days ago. ... The last one I received from
Angie was some two weeks ago. She told me about
Charley Mathers marriage and about Nelly Andrews
having an addition to the family and poor Julies wasted
charms and how can the men be so blind not to see
them and appreciate them, so they may. Tell her
that I love her and she cannot help herself. But I do
not want to marry, tell her.

    Dear Sisters Flum and Sharl try me and see if
I can't read your letters. Oh it would do me so much

good to get one from you. I will excuse your Dear letters Mother. I will answer all you write if it is every day and be glad to. Tell Father I would be glad to answer any from him but I receive none therefore I cannot answer any for him. I wish I could ...How is Caty[29] getting along? I wish you could keep her up home so that Sharl and Flum could have her to ride. I want them to learn to ride by the time I get home so they can go a Horseback riding with me. ... Tell Susan I will send her my likeness as soon as we get to a place I can get it taken.

Dear Mother, you and Father have yours taken and Sharll and Flums and tell father I will save money to pay for them. Oh what would we give to have Dear Jareds to look at now he is gone to return no more. I would give anything to have it but Dear Mother grieve not for him for happier far is he than we....Sixty cents a meal. ... Well I guess I will

---

[29] A horse.

take a meal when I come up that way. We live very well here but minus cake and pie. I go down to Jermans [Germans] close by when I get hungry for pie. They make very good pie for this outlandish country, people I mean.

Dear Mother, Father, and sisters I must bid you farewell for a while. Write soon. ... My best respects to my inquiring friends. Your humble but affectionate Son,

Ell.

Judson E. Miller, Co. L, 2rd Col. Cav. Jonhstown

In May Quantrill's raiders reappeared, attacked a Union forage wagon and its cavalry escort, killing one and wounding another. They burned the wagon and shot the mules, then cut the telegraph wire from Pleasant Hill to the Union headquarters. Three days later the raiders attacked the mail escort and captured the mail with all the departmental Union orders.

Some of Judson's mail was lost or destroyed in these events.

Harrisonville, Mo.   June 16th 1864

Dear Mother,

    ...We are back in Harrisonville again. We got back a week ago. ... It was so kind [of you] to send me the [news] paper. I had seen one paper that had an account of the Flood out of Denver. I was sorry to hear it. It must have been a sad sight to see the water coming down with such a rush carrying everything before it. Was I glad that you or any of the rest of them were not drounded [drowned]....

I expect we will stay here and not go back to Jonnstown [Johnstown]. We were getting things fixed up comfortable so we could enjoy ourselves first rate but we will be here the same. I board out to a good place. Most all the boys board out. Some pay 25 or 30 or 50c a week for having their rations cooked. Tell Sharll and Flum that six of our boys got married down in Jonstown. [Johnstown] Some of the girls was only thirteen or fourteen years old. Only think Sharll you are getting too old to marry down in this country, but there is time enough yet for you and Flum.

I have a good time ariding all over the country on a scout. I like it well and feel well.

The last weeks mail was robbed. I expect there was a letter or two for me in that mail.

There is some twenty of our boys down on the Osage River on a Scout some sixty miles from here. They have killed two bushwhackers and got some plunder that the bushwhackers had robbed some store of ... Write often direct to Kansas City. From your affectionate boy.

Ell.
J. E. Miller Co. L 2rd Col. Cav.

Harrisonville, Mo. Co. L 2nd Col Cav.

June 30th 1864

Dear Mother.

I received your long and kind letter of the 8th last night and it made me glad to hear that you are all well and this leaves me enjoying the same blessing. I had just come in from six days scout. I liked it first rate...No Mother I do not feel homesick but I want to come Home and see you all as bad as you want me to. I do not allow myself to get homesick and another thing I do not have time to.

Tell Father that I will write to him in a few days. I have not much to write this time and besides we are to have another inspection and mustered[30] in for pay day. We have not been paid off for the last four months. We have to muster every two months whether the paymaster comes or not and have our

---

[30] Muster is a mandatory assembly of troops.

arms inspected. My old carbine is a little rusty. I will have to rub a little of the rust off....It looks hard to see so many fine orchards going to ruin and this Fall when the grass and weeds get dry and the prairie gets afire it will sweep everything before it, houses, orchards, fences everything that is left. That is where no one is living. The only way we can get rid of these dam Bushwhackers is to remove the loyal people and then devastate and lay the country to waste and then just shoot down every dam last Rebel or simpathizers. [sympathizers] They have been here too long. The oath is nothing to them.[31] What do they care. They can take the oath and draw rations and be protected by both parties. They can live in the country and farm without fear and give the bushwhackers all the information they want in regards to our movements. The officers is to [too] easy with them. Oh if our soldiers had the privlige

---

[31] An oath of allegiance to the United States.

[privilege] we would soon clean them out. Mother I have got so I can see a Bushwhacker shot as well as a snake. Oh I hate them. Mother you have no idea how the Loyal people of Missouri has had to suffer by the dam Rebels. In the first outbreak of this rebellion the Rebs was the strongest party here. Most all the Loyal People were robbed of everything and most of them have had one or two of their men folk killed in cold blood by the trators [traitors]. I was at a place last night, Mr. Clevelands, where I get my washing done, they just received news that their only son was shot by the dam Rebels. The old man is very old and he lives in fear of his life. The men that were friends before the War are now deadly enemies. The old man said that the men that were his friends had told his daughter that they would kill her brother and her Father. They have killed her brother and her Father has to hide to save his life. Where I board, at Mr. Judges, he had his only two sons killed by the infernal dam Rebels. Oh Mother it is a horrible life to live. Oh I am glad you are not here.

You must excuse this poor letter. ...Good by this time. Tell Carv and Tood [32] that I will write soon, from your affectionate boy,

Ell

Judson E. Miller,

Co L, 2nd Co. Cav. Harrisonville, Cass Co. Mo.

---

[32] Judson's sister Susan.

Camp Waggoner, Little Blew [Blue] Mo.

August 18th 1864

Scharlott [Charlotte] Miller

Bare [Bear] Creek, Colorado

Dear Mother,

Yours of the 26th of July came to hand last night. It found me well and happy to hear from you. You see by the heading of this letter, Dear Mother, we have moved once more. We are camped on the little Blue[33] within six miles of Independence, eighteen miles of Kansas City and three miles from where Capt Waggoner was killed. His Company is here with ours. There are some other Gold Dirt boys in the Co. ... Stackhouse and one other man, I do not know his name, were killed in the fight with Waggoner. Tell Carve that Charlie Flanagan is dead.

---

[33] Little Blue and Big Blue Rivers are small tributaries of the Missouri. Both are in close proximity to the towns of Independence and Lexington.

We have a pleasant camp here. ...When we get in a place we do not like we are sure to stay some time but when we get in a place we like we do not stay long. We liked it fine at Harrisonville. Pleasant Hill I did not like. The latter place is some twenty miles from here due south, Harrisonville twelve miles southeast from there. We have a good time eating apples, melons, green corn and other good things. Independence is a very pirty [pretty] town. It has had the name of being the pirtiets [prettiest] town in the state. As the Missourian girl says, I ain't certain whether it is or not.

I wish we could come and kill those dam Indians. We are death to the Bushwhackers and I think we could play the Redskins a lively string. Are the people scared about the Indians getting to Denver? Angie said they were afraid of the Indians....

Tell Father that I would like to be there to help him get together the crops. I think that I have not forgotten how to work. But I am very lazy now. Tell Sharll and Flum I wish them to go to all the parties they can so when I get Home they can dance good. Because when I get Home we can go to every party there is going.

Yes Mother, I will take good care of myself. Every time we go out on a scout we have to [too] many for the Bushwhackers to show us a fight. They run every time we see one. They are too big cowards to pitch in on us unless they have three or five to one. They are worse than the Indians.

This leaves me well and hardy. Hoping this finds you enjoying the same blessing. I will close for this time. From you affectionate Son.

Judson E. Miller, Co L. 2rd Col. Cav., Direct to Kansas City

5. *The Dreaded Letter*

Letters coming home directly from soldiers were eagerly received. If the letter was from an officer it carried an ominous message. Early in October one such letter reached the Miller family in Denver.

The letter, from Captain Norton, was written to Judson's brother-in-law, Alex Atkins, who was married to Angeline (Annie or Angie) Miller and was the family member to be officially notified of Judson Miller's death. Atkins delayed passing the news to the rest of the family, hoping in some way to soften the impact of the news.

Independence Mo.   Oct 2nd 1884

[To,] Alex Atkins,

I do not know your Father-in-laws office address, I write to you. I have the sad and painful duty to inform you that our Dear Friend Judson E. Miller died this morning at 7 past 6 o'clock of hemorage of the stomach and bowel. He was sick not three days. My boys and myself with the attending physician done all we could to save his life, but it was all in vain. His Heavenly Father called for him and he must go. And we must soon follow him. May we so [endure] this deep affliction that we may be prepared when our Heavenly Father calls for us. We did not expect him to go so soon. In fact we did not look for him to die until it was too [late] with him in respect to sending any word to his family. I do not think he considered himself dangerously sick until he became unconscious.

Judson was beloved by all the Company Officers and men and they deeply feel his loss and we all deeply sympathize with you and his Dear Mother, Father and sisters. I fear it will almost break his Mother's heart but all must look to God for help to sustain us in these hours of darkness and trouble. We have a good black walnut coffin made for him and will bury him in his best Military Suit with Military Honors. We bury him at 3 this afternoon in the Independence burying ground close by the side of eight men of the 2nd Colorado who were killed with Capt Waggoner. The Regiment raised a fine marble monument which cost nearly $300 and stands at their heads. We put up a headstone with his name, age, day of death, and his Company and Regiment marked on it.

His account with the Government will be settled [by the] Adjutant General at Washington, to whom I send his final statement. What money he has together with his watch, pocket knife and gold pencil I will send by express to you that you may have some keepsakes of his. It will be a week or ten days before I send it as we are under marching orders and I can't attend to making out the proper papers for a few days. Any communication you wish to send me you will direct to Freeport, Stephenson Co. Ill. as I have resigned my Commission in the Army and it has been accepted. I return there. Lt. Holloway will be Captain in my stead. I have the honor to [be] yours,

Galen G. Norton,

Capt Co. L 2nd Colorado Cavalry

It then fell to Alex Atkins to inform the rest of Judson's family of the devastating news. The flowery language could not take away the impact.

Mr. Alanson Miller   Bear Creek.

Sir:

It has devolved upon me to forward you the accompanying painful intelligence which speaks too plainly to admit any ray of hope. Considering however that we too are mortal and must pass through the same transition in fulfilling our imortal destiny, and that death is only a portal to a brighter and happier world, we have even under the shadow of this bereavement an assurance that our loss is his immediate and permanent gain, that separation is but for a short season and when we are summoned to "shuffle off this mortal coil" we also shall be robed with him in the unchanging vestures of immortality.

The tribute which has been paid to Elliot by the officers and men of his company, is of itself a great consolation, and tho not killed in battle his life has no less been given for his country, and his resting place with that of the other departed with whose ashes he is now associated will ever be hallowed in our future history, whilst the monumental stone shall point out to future generations a spot sacred and revered from its association with the brave, the patriotic dead.

I write by this mail to Capt Norton returning our thanks for the kind care and attentions bestowed upon poor Elliot and for his expressions of sympathy contained in the letter herewith transmitted to you. So soon as the little mementos there in referred to shall arrive, I will haste to place them in your possession and if it is in my power to render any service in obtaining settlement of Elliot's a/c at Washington, commend me.

I have not yet communicated the sad news to Annie for the reason that her companion and neighbor Mrs. Cook *is far from home and without someone to bear her company and console with her the day would pass drearily indeed. Give my love to Mrs. M., Charlotte and Florence and believe me with deepest sympathy.*

Yours Truly

Alex W. Atkins

At the War's End

Like so many Civil War soldiers, Judson died not of wounds but by disease, which took more lives than bullets. He was 28 years old, one of the thousands of minor heroes of the time.

Within three weeks of Judson's death Confederate and Union troops were embroiled in what became known as the Second Battle of Lexington, a little river town only eight miles east of Independence. There two Union forces were poised to trap the Confederates, but many Kansas troops with past loyalties to the South refused to enter Missouri.

The battle see-sawed across the nearby Little Blue River, and the Confederates finally retreated. However, the five-hour battle took a heavy toll. The battlefields were littered with shattered wagons, broken guns, and 3,500 dead and wounded soldiers.

In a sense Judson's sickness and death three weeks earlier allowed him to escape the carnage.

When the war finally ended in April the following year, many of the guerilla fighters who initially refused the cease-fire finally decided to turn themselves in at Lexington. While riding into town they fought one more skirmish with Union soldiers. One of the guerillas, Jesse James, was severely wounded. Outraged, James returned to the outer world of banditry and continued to terrorize Western towns for decades.

Casualties during the Civil War are staggering. The official death count was 612,000.[34] Disease killed more than 620,000 and nearly half-million more were wounded.[35] The massive casualties resulted from the effectiveness of new weapons against old tactics, lack of camp sanitation, and minimal care for the wounded.[36]

---

[34] More than the total Americans killed in all wars prior to Vietnam.
[35] National Geographic Magazine, April 2005.
[36] Wikipedia – American Civil War.

The Family Carries On

After the death of both Miller sons, the family was discouraged. Sometime in 1865 the family outfitted a wagon train, intending to haul freight from Denver to Chicago. Alanson, his wife Charlotte, and their two unmarried daughters, Charlotte and Florence Cecilia, travelled east reaching Fremont, Nebraska where they stopped. Alanson had become very ill and did not recover. The family, all women, were stranded while a "friendly" co-traveler took the wagon train "on through to Chicago." The "friendly" co-traveler never returned.

The women were accomplished dressmakers and that provided their livelihood as they became respected townspeople. In 1873, the youngest daughter, Florence Cecilia, married Arundel C. Hull an early Western photographer, who had settled in Fremont after traveling and photographing the new Union Pacific Railroad alongside William H. Jackson.

Seven years after Judson's death his mother finally received his back pay.

**Judson's Mother in Her Later Years,
Charlotte Marshall Miller.**

**Judson' Sisters in the 1880s:
Florence, Cornelia, Susan, Charlotte, Angelina.**

Part II 1898
Runnie: A Nebraskan in Manila

Arundel Miller Hull

Arundel Miller Hull ("Runnie")

Born July 27, 1874, Fremont, Nebraska.

Enlisted May 3, 1898, Co. H, 1st Nebraska Volunteers.

Assigned to the Presidio, San Francisco, California for infantry training, promoted to Corporal.

Departed June 16, 1898 on SS *Senator*. Arrived Philippines July 18.

Promoted to Sergeant during the offensive against the Filipinos.

July 1899, departed Philippines on SS *Hancock* via Japan. Discharged San Francisco, August 23, 1899. Arrived Omaha, Nebraska August 30.

University of Nebraska, promoted to Cadet Major, R.O.T.C. Battalion. Graduated 1903 B.S. Electrical Engineering.

Married, 1906. Worked as a contractor installing municipal electrical plants, until contracting pneumonia in the spring 1911. Died July 5, 1911.

6. *Our Bellicose Imperialism*

The so-called "Spanish-American" War is a misnomer. It was a war with Spain, centered on colonial Cuba. Unexpectedly, it morphed into the Philippine-American War, a much minimized episode of bellicose imperialism in American history.

During the late 1890s there was growing unrest in Spanish colonial Cuba, and a civil war broke out between the native population and the increasingly repressive Spanish regime. The *insurrectos* attacked isolated Spanish outposts and burned sugar cane fields. Since Americans had nearly $50 million invested in those fields there was considerable American business interest in the goings on. In January 1898 the battleship USS *Maine* was sent to Havana, Cuba under the guise of a "courtesy call."

97

Library of Congress Spanish-American War website
USS *Maine.*

In reality, the USS *Maine* was sent to protect U.S. citizens and commercial interests there. In mid-February the USS *Maine* mysteriously blew up. The Spanish immediately launched efforts to rescue the survivors and disclaimed any responsibility for the event. However, the sensationalistic Hearst Newspapers attributed the blast to the Spaniards. William Randolph Hearst and Theodore Roosevelt's strident campaign helped galvanize the American public and led to a cry for war.

Decades later, in 1976, a more thorough non-political investigation concluded the explosion was due to spontaneous combustion in the coal bunker adjacent to a powder magazine. In 1999, another investigation (this one by the National Geographic Magazine) concluded it was most probably an underwater mine that set off detonation of the powder magazine. Nonetheless, the "Maine" incident served well as the justification for war with Spain.

Library of Congress Spanish-American War website
Wreckage of the USS *Maine* in Havana Harbor.

President McKinley initially resisted that cry for war, but in April, under great public pressure, he reluctantly sought and received congressional approval for sending troops to Cuba. Soon thereafter Spain declared war and the U.S. readily reciprocated.

In early July 1898 the U.S. Navy trapped the Spanish Atlantic Naval Squadron at Santiago, Cuba and destroyed it as it attempted a suicidal dash out of the harbor. Shortly afterward the U.S. landed ground forces east of the capitol, Santiago. The U.S. soon discovered the military tactics of the Civil War were not effective against the Spanish who had developed an effective strategy of concealment. The initial encounters with the Spanish resulted in embarrassing ambushes of U.S. troops.

Subsequent battles, although spotty, were more successful. A few weeks later, in the much celebrated battle of San Juan Hill, Teddy Roosevelt's "Rough Riders" fought their way toward Santiago only to be stopped short by 1,270 entrenched Spaniards. Fifteen thousand American troops laid siege and then successfully assaulted the city. More than 200 American soldiers were killed in the battle; however, far more casualties resulted from heat exhaustion and mosquito-borne disease.

In August, 109 days after the outbreak of war, a peace agreement ended the conflict. The Spanish were expelled from Cuba and the island was granted its independence. In the peace agreement the United States paid Spain nearly $20 million to acquire certain commercial and military rights in Cuba, gaining ownership of nearly all of the former Spanish colonies, notably Puerto Rico, Guam, and the Philippines.

In addition to military moves against Cuba, the U.S. dispatched warships and sent ground forces against Spanish Pacific colonies halfway around the world, primarily the Philippine Islands. Unaware of the peace accord, Commodore[37] Dewey's U.S. Asiatic

---

[37] Commodore Dewey was soon promoted to Admiral.

Squadron trapped the Spanish fleet at Luzon in Manila Harbor and proceeded to destroy it.

The war here was not ended however. The Spanish still occupied the islands and Dewey awaited the arrival of U.S. ground troops before attempting to drive them out.

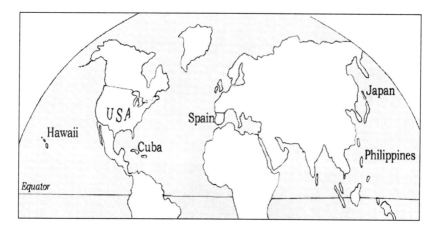

Map of the Northern Hemisphere.

The native Filipinos presented a complicating issue. During preceding years the natives had been fighting fiercely to gain their independence from Spain, but sporadic fighting had reached a stalemate. Lacking weapons and ammunition the revolutionaries, led by charismatic Emilio Aguinaldo, agreed to go into exile in Hong Kong for a payment of 800,000 pesos. (However, the Spaniards actually paid only half of it.)

When the U.S. declared war with Spain Aguinaldo's exiled regime was reinvigorated. In May 1898, one of Admiral Dewey' ships ferried Aguinaldo and his supporters from Hong Kong back to the Philippines assuming they would help oust the Spanish. In a few weeks the Revolutionary Philippine Army grew to nearly 12,000 troops. They held nearly all the ground within the Islands with exceptions of Manila itself and its immediate surroundings.

On June 12, 1898, Aguinaldo's revolutionaries declared Philippine independence, thus "officially" ending 333 years of Spanish rule.

Presidio Trust Museum

Emilio Aguinaldo, the Leader of the Philippine Revolutionary Army.

7. Patriotic Fervor at Home

Early in 1898 the prospect of war excited the entire nation. The country was anxious to exert our "Manifest Destiny."

On April 23rd President McKinley called for 125,000 volunteers to bolster the meager Regular Army. To avoid conflicts about authority over various states' widely divergent National Guard units, the Guard was federalized and volunteers were individually sworn in to federal service. War Department plans called for two volunteer infantry regiments from Nebraska. First Lieutenant John Stotsenburg[38], a Regular Army officer serving as Commander of Cadets at the University, was designated to organize the 1st Nebraska Volunteer Infantry. Companies were formed by recruits from each of the twelve larger Nebraska towns.

Arundel Miller Hull (Runnie) was in his sophomore year at the University of Nebraska, and was eager to go.

---

[38] Lieutenant Stotsenburg was soon to be promoted to Colonel.

Lincoln May 2, 1898

Dear "Dad" & "Ma,"

I received your letter yesterday. I have not gone in any company and did not intend to 'til after school was out, but they have orders to go to Omaha tomorrow at 10. There are 52 boys from the Univ that enlisted before yesterday and 18 more are going to enlist today. There is one company Co. H of Nelson that has 8 Univ. boys and Perry, the Capt of the Pershing Rifles[39] enlisted in that company and he said "If you enlist, come with me." I know what that means for he has his name before the officers at Washington as an army man and has the commission of "Cap" in the volunteer Co. If you think that it would be all right for me to go in that company, I would like to. If mama makes any fuss about or would not feel alright if I go, why I don't want to go. If she will take it good naturedly, wire Yes and if there is any trouble wire No.

The commandant says one Regiment goes to the Forts in Neb & the other to the coast. They may be in Omaha a month yet. I will be thinking about it 'til I get your answer[40]. Run

---

[39] The Pershing Rifles is an honorary drill team selected from members of the R.O.T.C.
[40] Apparently one of these letters conveyed his parents' consent to enlist.

Runnie Signs Up

After an exchange of letters with his parents in Fremont, he got their acquiescence to volunteer. On May 3rd he signed up with Company H, along with several of his fellow students and on May 9, 1898 the 1st Nebraska Volunteer Infantry Regiment was formally mustered into service at Lincoln. The regiment was composed of twelve companies organized into three battalions.

After about a week in which they were partially outfitted, the new regiment boarded two troop trains for San Francisco. Company H traveled through Hastings, Cheyenne, and Reno where the train was held up while a wreck was cleared. Sabotage was excitedly, but mistakenly, rumored.

Along the way crowds warmly greeted the new soldiers and during their Reno stop the recruits were given a few hours "run of the town." Back on board the troop trains, they passed through Sacramento and on to San Francisco. After crossing the Bay they gathered their gear and marched five miles across the city to their camp site adjoining the Presidio.

When these recruits arrived in San Francisco, the First Expedition to the Philippines, carrying already organized units from California and Oregon, had departed a few days earlier. The Nebraskans were slated to be part of the Second Expedition.

Florence Hull, Runnie's Mother.

After Runnie arrived in San Francisco his first long letter home was to his mother.

San Francisco, June 8, 1898

Dear Mom

I received your letter quite a while ago and a number from "Pa" but I don't have ... much time.

We are having a pretty good time but we have to drill hard. We drill out northwest of camp in some hilly ground near the mouth of the Golden Gate about a mile from it. We can see some of the big guns lined up along each side of the water. The Neb boys were the first ones here at the camp. There are about 15,000 here now from different states.

The people here are very nice but they don't seem to know much or they think we are awful green. They talk as though Neb was a very poor country and one fellow asked one of our boys if he ever heard of San Francisco before we came here.

The Red Cross societies and other people bring us pies and cakes etc. once in a while.

Our camp is west of the city and is in the place where the old Bay District race track used to be. Just south of here about 3 blocks is the Golden Gate Park and beyond that are 3 Univ buildings built not long ago . . . .

A few days ago we were vaccinated (it was last Sunday) and today I am feeling sick as are a few others. . . . I think in about 2 weeks or less we will be sicker.

One of our Regiment Lieutenants and 14 men were guarding the ship that is to take the Neb boys to Manila. It is taking on supplies and being fixed up, and we are to be ready Tuesday and sail Wed.

I suppose we will be over there nearly two years but I can take care of myself that long I guess. I have not been sick here but today all of the others in my tent have. This country here is no good. It is so hot, about 3 days that we have to go in our shirt sleeves and there for about a week it is measly. It doesn't rain but it would be better if it did. It is foggy. We are right in the clouds all of the time. They don't call it rain but we get it just the same and it is cold too. A very unhealthy place. Maybe you don't believe it but it is just the same. Why Neb has the best climate by far.

I received that little picture. It is all right. Well, I suppose you know I did not get transferred to Co. B but I got a corporately in this company.

Well I guess I will get my pay tonight so tomorrow I will have my mug taken if someone comes around.

I will write again before I go.

Run

To accommodate the rapidly arriving recruit volunteers a temporary tent camp was set up south of the Presidio just outside of the Arguello Gate. Camp Merritt[41] had been hurriedly set up on the windy, foggy site of the old Bay District Racetrack. The ground covered with loose sand, full of fleas, and difficult to walk in was not a popular place.

---

[41] Camp Merritt was named for Major General Wesley Merritt, commander of the Army's Department of the Pacific.

Food preparation facilities and sanitation for the several thousand volunteer troops who occupied the camp was ill-conceived and poorly organized.

Sgt. Hiram Harlow Collection, Presidio Trust Library

Camp Merritt, San Francisco Presidio, 1898.

During Camp Merritt's short existence disease and sickness were widespread. With an "open" camp many of the local prostitutes brought along venereal disease. The persistent dampness brought on bronchitis and pneumonia, and the poor sanitary facilities brought on cases of typhoid and dysentery.

Because so many of the volunteers became ill an Army General Field Hospital was established in the permanent brick barracks inside the Presidio.

San Francisco, Cal. June 11, '98

Dear "Dad"

We just got paid off a little while ago. We got paid for two months, one month in advance. I received $31.52. One month's pay as a private and one as a corporal. I don't think I will use this money so I will send $20 home.

I think it is a sure thing that we go now. We will probably sail on the "Senator."

If you notice the Neb State Journal of June 7, you will see quite a piece by one of the boys in our tent. He is a nice young fellow, very smart and acts as stenographer at Headquarters.

Yesterday evening we had Dress Parade and this morning inspection by Gen'l Green. [42]

My arm is stiff and I have been in my tent a little sick since I wrote last but I am all right now. I hope vaccination is a good thing part of the time. You know "Mom" said the other time it made me sick. Nearly all of the boys have gone down town for we get 'til eight o'clock without anything to do today.

[42] Brigadier General Francis V. Greene, 2nd Expedition Commander.

Probably some few will drink nearly all of their money up but take the Reg. as a whole I know that there are fewer drunks than in any other Regiment here except maybe the Iowa boys for they came in yesterday and so I can't tell about them. The few that have been drunk here were given hard punishment.

In our company is a Hall who has deserted 2 times and once for 10 days at a time. If you hear about it don't think it is a Hull. There are three Hulls so when I hear my name I don't turn around 'til someone hits me.

Today we had a meeting to form a society or the like to see about and tend to the company's business outside of the military post and I was chosen president.

We won't see any more pay 'til Sept and maybe I will need the money so I will not send any this time. Well, I will stop. If I am too late for the P. O. then I will send it tomorrow.

Runi   Co. H, 1ˢᵗ Neb Vol.

June 15   On the Senator

Dear "Dad"

We left camp yesterday PM and were given a feed by the ladies of the Red Cross Societies about supper time and then put on the "Senator."

Had good night's rest as the boat was standing steadily in Dock No. 11. We will be here a day or so I guess but will leave soon.

I hear that we will stay just a while in Honolulu.

The whole Neb. reg. is on this boat.

I think I will be back in 2 years when the rest come back so good bye. All keep well and I will do the same.   Run.

After a modicum of training, the Nebraskans boarded the SS *Senator*, a relatively small chartered steamer that had been hurriedly outfitted as a troop transport. They departed June 15 as part of the Second Expedition.

The men were assigned to bunks in tight rows three and four tiers high. They were, as described by one of them, "packed in like hogs in a pen." But it was better than the camp at San Francisco. Since it was quite hot in the compartments below, many men preferred to sleep on deck. For most of the Nebraskans this was their first experience aboard ship and predictably many of them suffered from seasickness. There was also an outbreak of measles and one case of fatal spinal meningitis.

Courtesy of Nebraska State Historical Society

SS *Senator* with Nebraska Troops Crowding the Deck.

Nine days out of San Francisco the troop ships steamed into the harbor at Honolulu to take on coal. For a day and a half the soldiers enjoyed the "finest island in the world." After leaving Honolulu seasickness again became widespread and a measles outbreak filled up the dispensary.

International Date Line was a bit of a puzzler when they crossed it on June 30. July 1st disappeared and the next day was July 2.

After leaving Honolulu, the Second Expedition stopped briefly at Wake Island. General Green with a small landing party went ashore to seize it. The "seizure" amounted to reading a proclamation and raising the American flag on a rusty flagpole near the center of the unoccupied island.

It was America's second Pacific "conquest." The first had occurred a few days earlier, on June 20, when the cruiser USS *Charleston* fired a few rounds on the Spanish fort at Guam. The island's commander had not yet been informed of Spain's surrender and misunderstood the firing as a salute. He signaled his regrets and that he was unable to return the salute because he had no ordnance.

As the Expedition steamed on westward, target practice gave the men a chance to break their boredom. Floating targets were towed behind the steamers and the troops were allowed a few shots with their obsolete Springfield single-shot rifles.

On the SS *Senator*, Runnie and the other Nebraskans were unaware of the high anxiety on another of the transports. A fire broke out in one of the coal holds and fighting the fire caused the ship to list. On one side the passengers could see nothing but water, on the other, nothing but sky.[43] (The fire was finally extinguished when the Expedition arrived in Manila harbor.)

———————————————

[43] Linn, B. M., The Philippine War 1899-1902, p.15.

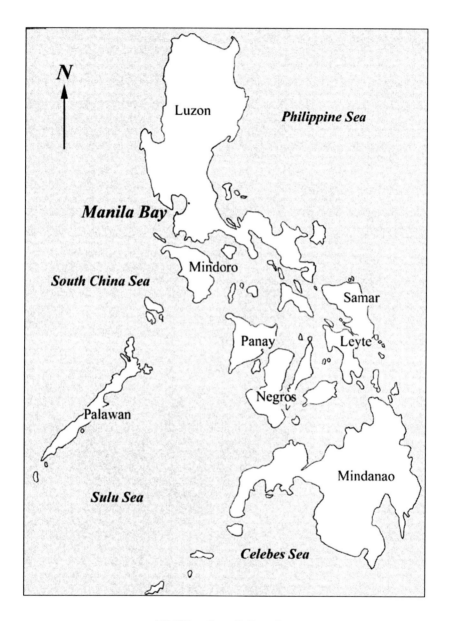

Philippine Islands.

In the Philippines

Since Manila harbor was unusable, the American ships anchored at Cavite, a small harbor about twenty miles south of Manila. There the First Expedition had just finished off-loading troops and their equipment. The Second Expedition followed suit. Landing was a slow process with small native boats shuttling across shallow water between anchored ships and the shore. Once ashore troops formed up and moved along the shoreline to join earlier arrivals at the primary encampment, Camp Dewey, about five miles outside the city.

The Manila Bay Vicinity.

8. Letters From the Philippines, 1898

To the Nebraskans everything was new. The tropical climate, especially the temperature and rain, was quite a change from dry Nebraska. The natives were quite different from the American Indians back home and, of course, languages were a challenge.

WITH THE FIRST NEBRASKA

Runnie Hull of This City Writes an Interesting Letter.

TELLS OF LIFE AT CAMP DEWEY.

Just Like Camping Out and About as Enjoyable—Is Not Much Hotter Than in Nebraska—The Boys are all In Good Health.

Mr. and Mrs. A. C. Hull received a letter yesterday from their son, Runnie, who is with Co..11, 1st Nebraska regiment at Manila. It is the first received from him since the regiment went into camp. THE TRIBUNE has been given permission to publish parts of it:

CAMP DEWEY, Manila, July 27.

Fremont Tribune

Camp Dewey, July 27, 1898

To the Family,

I wrote from Honolulu and also a letter last week before we landed. Did you get them?

We arrived in the harbor on the [July] *18th and came ashore on the 20th. Our camp is about 4½ miles from Manila and about a half a mile in from the shore. Our tents are pitched in a garden patch which is about 2 blocks wide and 2 mi long.*

All around the place the natives have built their houses in the trees and brush. Most of them at the north end, and forming sort of a town, and along the road just east of us. It rains about twice a day and rain or shine the natives are lined up with their baskets of fruit etc. just outside of the guard line.

Our tents are small and made up of two parts that button together. Two men sleep in a tent and each carries half when on the march. My tent mate, Bert Stoner and I raised our tent up about a foot or more and put in a bed that a native made of bamboo. The other fellows have raised their tents also but believe ours is the best.

Nina Hull Miller Collection

Company H Camp Street.

Our whole trip from start to now has been a picnic; of course on the ship was crowded but that was nothing. Now while we are here it seems just like camping out. It is not much hotter than where you are. We get wet and when the sun comes out everything gets dry again. If it rains long like it has been doing today our drills are suspended and the fellows take to their tents. It is raining now and I am in my tent with my dry underclothes on. I have to take my wet clothes off and as soon as the sun comes out I'll dry 'em up.

Part of the 3rd Expedition came in day before yesterday and the rest will be in soon. The insurgents have driven the [Spaniards] to within a short distance from Manila. About every morning the natives make an attack and two or three times since we have been here they have passed with prisoners. They say the "Americano" are lazy because we do not fight.

The companies change off so that there are always 2 companies on outpost duty every day. Roads are being cut through the timber and bridges are being constructed. Our boys are making a wharf about half a block long near our camp.

The officers think that we will take the whole thing without any "scrapping" at all. – I mean Manila.

Dewey took in some mutton that some ship tried to run in to Manila, so we get a little extra for meals now. We do not get so very much to eat or of a different variety but everything is good and just about enough.

To be sure of our water we boil it and I have the honor of seeing that it is boiled. Companies G and H have dug a well in their cook tents and it is all right. It is about 8 feet deep with a barrel in the bottom to keep out dirt. The water is clear and cool but we boil it anyway. Well I've got to mail this right away.

Next time I will write more. I'm well and having a good time.

Run   *Co. H I^st Neb, U. S. V.*

Nina Hull Miller Collection

Cook Tent Company H.

After his cheery letter of July 27, Runnie did not write home for several weeks. In November he reported on the events that kept him very busy during the summer and fall, and of the increasing tension between the Filipino Guerillas and the American troops.

An Independent Nation or "Colony"?

As the American troops arrived in significant numbers, tensions grew between them and the Revolutionary Philippine forces. Aguinaldo felt his people were betrayed, having believed that the Americans would help their cause for independence. Not so it turned out. The Americans viewed the islands as theirs now, a "colony," ready for "development" or exploitation.

In past decades the Spanish had built a series of stone Block Houses around the perimeter of Manila to defend against random raids by *insurrectos*. Now, as the Spanish retreated into the city, they also occupied most of the Block Houses and continued their stiff resistance, well aware of their fate if the insurgents were to gain the upper hand.

Courtesy of Nebraska State Historical Society
Block House 7.

Aguinaldo's insurgent troops entirely surrounded the city, keeping the Americans outside their lines. The Americans were likely to be thwarted in any attempt to capture and occupy the city. General Greene, through skillful negotiations, persuaded the Filipino general commanding the insurgent troops near Camp Dewey to move his soldiers aside so that the Americans could occupy a narrow corridor between the harbor and the inland swamp land.

In several of Runnie's letters he would catch up on reports of his activities, always trying to reassure those at home of his well being. The following is from his next letter.

Nina Hull Miller Collection
Utah Battery at Drill.

July 30. We went on "outpost" duty it was the first time - we were new at the business. One night before the regulars had moved forward a number of hundred yards and thrown up the breast works.[44] When we got there we had to trot in under fire but the bullets were too high. The firing was kept up a little all day while we raised the earth works from a little over knee high to nearly as high as our chin. Next morning early the Utah battery moved in and about that time a few shells came our way and bullets came close. The Pennsylvania boys came and relieved us soon. That night (31st) at 11 o'clock they were attacked in the breastworks. All troops in camp were called out and stood in the rain for an hour. Firing ceased and company dismissed.

On Aug. 2 Neb went out on outpost again. The first time we were up in the entrenchments near the beach by the old church. This time we were the "reserves" and stationed about a mile back of the entrenchments with the companies some distance apart. Called into line about 10 o'clock at night, firing all along the front. Bullets and shells came down by us. At one o'clock at night we were called out again and all sent to the

---

[44] Breastworks are mounds of earth, sandbags, logs or any other material that could afford protection from enemy fire.

front. Firing stopped soon after the time we started and we had to lay in the mud and water 'til 9 the next morning without getting a shot or two for our trouble.

Aug 6. We went out again and held down the works on the extreme right which ended at a swamp and crossed a road leading to Manila. In the middle of the night firing began. I and my squad were out ahead and had orders to come in when an attack was made. We got in and crouched down behind the works with the others. The orders were not to fire 'til the command was given and as no approach was made on us we did not get a chance to fire.

Aug. 7. Transports moved people from Manila and no fighting was going on.

Aug 9. We went out on post again near the old church or cathedral. It was quiet all day and night not a shot fired by either side. On the days we were not out in the entrenchments or were on outpost, we spent the time washing our muddy clothing, sleeping and drilling. We wanted all the sleep we could get for it is no easy job to stay up all night in the wet and sloppy trenches.

The Spanish trapped within the city were without hope. The water supply had been closed off and food supplies bottomed out. Early in August, Admiral Dewey and General Merritt demanded that the Spanish Governor General surrender the city. The Governor could not do so without consulting the authorities in Madrid. Unfortunately, he could not do that either, the Americans having purposely severed the transoceanic telegraph cable under Manila Bay, their primary communication line.

Nina Hull Miller Collection

Troops Watch the Shelling.

After a series of somewhat ambiguous negotiations, Dewey and Merritt came to an "understanding" with the Spanish Governor General.

To avoid torture and execution by the rebels the Spaniards would surrender only to the Americans. After a brief skirmish the Americans would assist them to escape the island.

Mid-morning on August 13th Admiral Dewey's warships commenced firing on Manila starting with Fort Malate at the southern edge of the city.

Nina Hull Miller Collection

Ruins From Dewey's Shelling.

The Spanish had conveniently vacated the fort and removed their cannon. The American ground troops advanced from their positions near Camp Dewey and under scattered fire reached and entered the city.

The Nebraskans advanced along the shoreline in front of the old walled city and took a position near the Customs House. By evening the Spanish surrendered to the Americans and the city was in American hands.

Courtesy of Nebraska State Historical Society
1st Nebraska Wading Along Seawall.

During the next few days the Spanish forces were allowed to board their ships and depart. The Filipinos were understandably furious.

It was two more months before Runnie wrote again. He was then in a momentary "sight-seeing mode."

Manila, Aug. 27, 98

To the Family,

You know before now that the city of Manila now belongs to Uncle Sam, in other words we have taken the place; and did not have a very hard time either.

Friday night the 12th of [August] the Captain came down the street in front of our tents and told us all that the next morning at 11 o'clock there would be a general attack on Manila by land and by sea. We all expected this would come soon and I think everybody was ready at the next morning. We cleaned up our tents and folded blankets and put everything in good shape at camp and started out at 8 o'clock with 2 days rations and 200 rounds of ammunition.

Our regiment was stationed near the beach and about a mile back of the entrenchments. Other troops were stationed in the roads on our right and many in the entrenchments.

We waited 'til half past ten when the ships began their work. Only three ships and a small dispatch boat, the Callao, fired away. I think they were the Olympia, Boston and Raleigh. Not very big guns were used but in the short half hour that the small ones were used the Spanish in front of us got aplenty.

They expected us to attack with greater force along a road just at our right and had placed a great many soldiers behind the works at the end of the road. One 6 in. shell went through there and exploded and those not injured could not be held back. The works in front of us were battened down and soon fell back to the main walls except in front of the boys away over on the right.

The little Callao moved close into shore and peppered 7 pounders and lead of different sizes from its 10 rapid firing guns and did good work.

After firing ceased the troops moved forward. The Neb boys took the beach and had easy marching 'til we got to the river, from there on we waded along the beach. A stone wall on the edge of the bay kept us out in the water which was most often waist deep.

The Spanish had been driven from here by the ships guns so that we had no trouble in moving forward. We were fired on occasionally by their rear guard but it was high.

Just across the river the band stopped and played "A Hot Tune" as we passed. We had nothing to stop us and some got in the city before the advance guards of the other regiments and nearly cut off some of the retreating soldiers.

Well we ate supper in Manila and are here yet and I suppose good for 3 months more.

The different regiments are stationed around at different places all over town. The Neb regiment has 2 large buildings and 2 or 3 small ones. We are not very far from the mouth of the Pasig River.

I received your and Charlie's letters quite a while back. Today I received your letter and paper.

We drill 3 times a day and are not permitted to go out of our barrax [barracks] except at certain times. I have taken in the town a little and find a great many curious things.

I am well and getting along all right, don't have very much time because the hot climate makes a fellow need sleep and I use up half the afternoon that way. We get good grub and the only thing I kick on is the bed, our blankets are on the floor. The floor is of good solid mahogany plank with the hard side up.

Well I'll have to stop. I will write again soon.
Run

Tensions escalated as the Filipinos cut off the water supply and refused to restore it without concessions from General Merritt.

To compound matters the American generals were exposing their egos and were bickering between themselves.

Meanwhile, conditions within the city were deteriorating for the troops: bad food, inadequate sanitation, and infected quarters. Typhus, malaria, and dengue fever spread through the city's fouled sewers and backwaters.

Nina Hull Miller Collection

Troopers Cleaning Up Their Quarters On the Pier.

The Nebraskans were quartered in a dank warehouse on the Manila docks, where the men slept on wet floors, with no place to eat except on the streets or in their bunks, no washing facilities, and inadequate sanitation. By mid-October, six Nebraskans had died and seventy-eight were so sick they were recommended for early discharge.[45]

Nina Hull Miller Collection

Troopers Setting Up Quarters.

By some good fortune Runnie soon moved to better quarters. He escaped illness, or at least he did not write about it.

---

[45] Linn, B. M. p. 31.

POST CARD   Manila, 10-18-98

Dear Dad

Everything all right. Health good. "Chip off the old block." I and another of this Company are making pictures. We cannot get all the right stuff here. If we are to be here for 3 months or more after you get this, you would probably know. Please send me 1 doz. rolls of film 2 ½ x 3 ¼ for Eastman Folding Kodak, and paper for 1,000 prints, and get the formula for the best toning solution for that paper. We would like paper that does not need ice water. Make the package tight. Do not send it unless you know we will be here long enough to use it. Send the bill.

Our battalion could not ask for better quarters. I will write soon. We can get everything but paper and film.

Run   Co H, 1st Neb Vol. Manila P. I.

Manila, Nov. 17, 1898

Dear "Mom"

I received papers and a letter from Pa yesterday; he said you people had not heard from me since July 7. Well, I thought I wrote later than that.

But I wrote some between about the 1st. of August and the time we entered Manila.

I will write from some notes I have and tell what happened then.

And here we are in Manila yet. Maybe you will think that I am not in it when I tell you I did not fire a shot all through this but I guess I was. It happened that our company every time had to be blazed at and not do a thing but take it.

Some day soon I'll write more. I am well

Runi

Perhaps you have read in the Popocratic[46] Sheet of Lincoln [Nebraska] *about bravery of our Cap. and the cowardly stragglers in our company. Well there were no stragglers and you can guess the rest.*

- - -

The "Loco"

A "Care" Package From Home

Some of the folks at home realized it would take a while for Christmas packages to reach Manila before the holidays. Thus a special effort was launched by a group in Nelson, Nebraska.

---

[46] Popocrates (Populist-Democrats) were a political party in the late 1800s.

NOTICE
NEBRASKA'S SPANISH-AMERICAN WAR RELATIVES' UNION
NELSON, NEBRASKA, OCTOBER 18, 1898.

The friends of the soldier boys now in the field have organized the Spanish-American War Relatives' Union for the purpose of looking after the welfare of the soldiers away from their homes. To the end, that arrangement may be made with the War Department whereby donations from friends may be transported to their camps and the same shall be prepared so that they reach the boys on or before Christmas so that this arrangement may be completed and each company and soldier receives his gifts at the same time.

The donations for the boys in the 1st Regiment must be prepared at once so as to reach them at Manila by Christmas and must be shipped by November 15. The friends of the boys at each home station must organize and communicate with me at once.

BOXES
Each soldier should be sent a box not larger than 18 inches length, 8 inches wide, and 8 inches deep made of pine. These dimensions should be followed when possible for convenience of repacking in shipping case, which should be made of good inch pine lumber, well bound, and lined on the inside with waterproof building paper. The small boxes will have the name and company of the soldier it is intended for; the packing case, name of the company and regiment plainly marked. Notify me when it is ready to ship.

CONTENTS OF BOX

Of course, persons are permitted to enclose in the boxes what they choose. It is suggested, however that, owing to the distance, change of climate, and length of time occupied by shipment, care should be taken that nothing whatever be sent of a perishable nature. Of edibles, fruit cakes, preserves, jellies or any canned goods may be sent, but no fruit or cooked food of any kind other than that named above should be included, for the reason that it would not only spoil, but would taint other articles contained in the large package. Clothing and trinkets of any kinds may be sent safely.

I suggest that each box might contain 2 undershirts, all wool; 2 pairs of drawers, all wool; 6 cotton stockings, 6 colored handkerchiefs; 6 medium size Turkish towels, hair brush, comb, tooth brush, one dozen needles, one spool of black linen thread, one dozen pants buttons, one dozen pearl shirt buttons, one small pin cushion and pins, one dozen stamped envelopes, six of them directed to the mother or dear friend of the soldier, one quart of home-made pickles, one quart of cherries, one pound of fruit cake, one pint of grated horseradish.

The members of the G. A. R. are expected to lend a helping hand. Who knows better than they the benefits derived from such work?[47]

James D. Gaye, Assistant Adjutant General

---

[47] The Hull family, like many others, dutifully packed a box and sent it off to a lady in Nelson, Nebraska who was consolidating a shipment to the soldiers of Company H. The shipment reached the soldiers in early March.

Nelson Nebraska Nov 6, 1898

Mr. A. C. Hull,

Your box came safely to Nelson, but was here repacked in a tin box. Tin boxes are chosen because all articles are sure to be preserved in them, and after being filled will be soldered up tight and names painted on outside.

My father and mother Mr. and Mrs. C. R. Stoner, opened and repacked the box you sent. As the tin boxes were larger than the one you sent, there was some extra space which I filled with some fruit cake and a small feather pillow which I had intended sending to your son by mail. Also we took the liberty of putting in another small pillow for my brother A. J. Stoner. We have a special interest in your boy. He was so good and kind to my brother when sick in San Francisco. Bert sent us Mr. Hull's picture so we feel that we know him. Since leaving San Francisco, Bert and your son have tented together.

The tin box had to be of a uniform size for convenience in packing into the larger packing cases. You will readily understand that it was necessary to repack your box, and we hope you will not think we took too great a liberty with private property.

Sincerely, Lauretta S. Newton

9. A Different War Erupts

During January 1899 the tense conditions between the American troops and Filipinos began to escalate with occasional pot shots at each other.

In December the 1st Nebraska Volunteers moved out of Manila to the newly created Camp Santa Mesa east of the city. The San Juan River makes a curving meander around three sides of the camp which made it somewhat precarious. The American troops patrolled the camp perimeter and occupied a series of outposts. However, the Filipinos were in close proximity, occupying the higher surrounding ground. They also occupied nearby Block Houses 6 and 7.

Courtesy of Nebraska State Historical Society
Camp Santa Mesa.

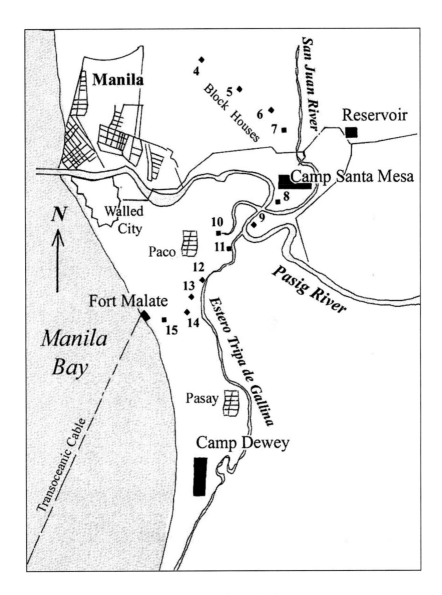

Manila and Vicinity.

Nina Hull Miller Collection
San Juan Bridge Near Camp Santa Mesa.

In the early evening of February 4th two American sentries stood on outpost duty guarding the nearby San Juan River Bridge. As they rested they heard a soft whistle and spotted two shadowy Filipino soldiers moving across the bridge into the American-held territory. After the Filipinos ignored the sentry's challenge, a single shot killed one of them and immediately triggered a shower of return fire.

The American sentries guarding the bridge retreated a short distance to take cover behind the pipeline. Shortly, they were joined by thirty additional troops, the entire outpost.

In fifteen minutes firing spread around the entire city perimeter from Caloocan at the north to Fort Malate on Manila Bay to the south. It was now open warfare and although somewhat disorganized it was no longer the Spanish-American War; it was now the Philippine-American War.[48]

Nina Hull Miller Collection
Troopers on the Highway to Pasay.

---

[48] Thiessen, T. D., The Fighting First Nebraska, p. 235.

Nina Hull Miller Collection
Troopers on the Firing Line at Pasay.

Feb 8, 1899

Dear Father,

This letter will not get to you 'til the news is old but I might as well tell you about our scrap.

Early Sat night [Feb 4] trouble started between the outposts and the whole regiment was called out and companies placed in the best possible places. Our company [Co. H] was stretched out along the water pipe north of camp. Here we got fire from the front and down the pipe from the bridge on the right and all that came over camp.[49] The lead came thick too, or rather Mauser bullets, but we had the pipe in front

[49] Camp Santa Mesa.

and an embankment behind. Fire lasted all night but not continuously.

Next morning the work started. A company of Nebraska and some Colorado on our left moved over to a block house[50] after the Utah battery pounded into it, and captured it after a hard scrap.

At the same time Co. H had started toward the bridge. We crossed the bridge and captured the powder magazine and a couple of block houses around but it took time and hard work. We were fired on [from] all sides but the rear and they kept it up as they retreated from one stone wall and hill to another but it was too high. Ours was high enough for every now and then we heard the command "fire low boys." It took us 'til noon to get to the reservoir but we got there and [captured] it too. We left a big path [of casualties] that [have] not all been buried yet.

We stayed at the reservoir 'til next day and then started for the water works. We fought our way there but we got there just the same, and this morning our company came back to this place, half way between the W. W. and reservoir.

---

[50] Block House 7.

There are 4 large pumps (all fly wheel) and 4 boilers, made by Merleese, Tait and Watson of Glasgow in 1881.[51]

Well it is easier to write than to scrap but I guess I have to stop. Everything quiet now but all around town Uncle Sam's boys had the same trouble we did.

Nebraska lost 8 and 20 wounded. I'm all right

Run

Nina Hull Miller Collection
Artillery Clearing the Woods Near Pasay.

---

[51] Runnie and his father shared a special interest in public utilities, water-works, and electrical systems.

FREMONT BOY IN THE FIGHT

Runnie Hull Writes of the

Fight With Insurgents

NEBRASKA LADS HAD PLENTY TO DO

A Rain of Lead from Three Sides When They Charged --- Took Everything They Went After --- Was One of the Fortunate Ones Who Was Not Hurt --- What a Manila Paper Says of the First Nebraska's Fighting Material.

Yesterday afternoon A. C. Hull received a letter from his son Runnie with Company H First Nebraska. It was dated February 8th, which was only a few days after the fight with the insurgents. He reported himself as coming out all right and gives a brief account of his part in the engagement which was in substance as follows:

Fremont Tribune

The hometown paper reprinted Runnie's letter of February 8 and an article from the Manila paper.

Manila Paper Praises Nebraskans

The "American," a paper published in Manila has been received in this city, and it praises the work of the First Nebraska regiment in the highest terms. Following is a part of an article in the edition of February 8th on the First Nebraska:

The boys from Nebraska have been called "pumpkin rollers," but …. they proved conclusively they could roll lead as swiftly and accurately as any of the troops now in the field. … The way they gave the insurgents a hot time … made the Nebraska boys envied of all troops on the east side of the city. They were strictly in it from start to finish. They started ahead of any other regiment and continued long after the others had finished.

The trouble started by the insurgents trying to bring a number of their men across the San Juan Bridge. As this was in defiance of previous agreement … the sentries objected to any interference from the insurgents. The latter then returned and securing a stronger force, tried to take possession of the bridge.

Colonel Stotsenburg quickly had the entire regiment to support the outpost and drove the insurgents to their own line. The block houses were then cleared and captured in the most brilliant manner. Following up their success the Nebraska boys went after the fort and powder magazine which was in the rear of the block houses.

Here they were most stubbornly opposed, and in the face of a terrific fire advanced to the opposite slope and successfully carried out their work.

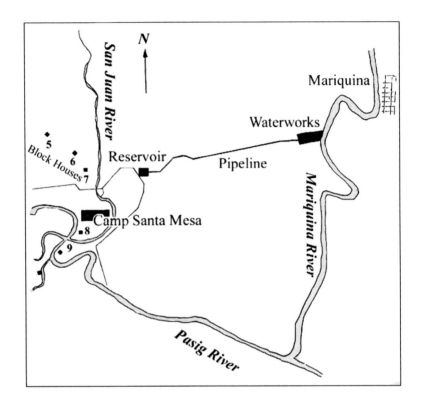

Manila Waterworks.

Up along the pipeline a Nebraska patrol was fired on from the town of Mariquina. Reinforced, the Nebraskans drove the insurgents from the village and as retaliation, but contrary to the prevailing Field Orders, the village was set afire. The conflict was growing ever more intense.

The Skirmishes Continue

After fighting all the way along the pipeline to the river the Nebraskans discovered the pumps at the waterworks had been disabled and sabotaged.[52] The Filipinos had removed the big pump heads, and other engine parts, rendering them inoperable. The parts were completely missing. The troops searched nearby fields and dragged the muddy river without success. A detachment of machinists quickly came out from Manila and measured up the pumps intending to manufacture replacement parts in the shops at Cavite. Meanwhile, during a renewed search, one of the troopers noted a curious pile of dirt inside a coal shed. After digging a three-foot-deep pit they found the missing parts each covered with a protective coating of white lead. Within a day the parts were cleaned up, the pumps reassembled, and rapidly put back in service, fortunately without seriously restricting the water supply to the city.

It was almost a month before Runnie wrote again. During that time the Nebraskans were spread out from the waterworks about five miles back to the reservoir and Camp Santa Mesa. Sporadic fighting persisted all along the pipeline, keeping the soldiers constantly on edge.

---

[52] Hunt, G. H., Colorado's Volunteer Infantry in the Philippine Wars, p. 166.

In some areas fighting was continuous along the pipeline. Troops were called out repeatedly; there were eight engagements in a twenty-three day period.

Nina Hull Miller Collection

Six Troopers – Arundel Hull Is Front and Center.

In the city of Manila itself the Provost Guard, being spread thin, found it increasingly difficult to maintain order. Knife-wielding assailants roamed about, snipers took pot shots, and buildings were torched. In Paco, a suburb to the south, a clandestine gun powder factory exploded, setting a fire that burned much of the town. At the same time large areas of Manila were torched, setting off street battles, rampant looting, and destruction of many buildings.

With the growing turmoil the city became almost as hazardous as the battleground. Several companies of the Volunteer troops were assigned to reinforce the Provost Guard and a two-week street battle ensued. Over 100 revolutionary sympathizers and looters were arrested and the insurgents driven out of the city. They were momentarily defeated and demoralized.

Manila P. I. At Camp Dinger ......March 6, '99

Dear Father and the Others.

We got our Christmas boxes three days ago and don't you forget it was a treat to us all. Mrs. Stoner my tent mate's mother added some cake and candied fruit and preserves. For these and what my own folks sent I am very thankful. Everything comes in handy and hits the right spot.

Yesterday we had trouble right after dinner.

Mr. Treen was with us. We got out our Christmas boxes and had a great time. He said, "Say this is better than I ever get in town." After dinner came the "Call to Arms," and he got a gun and ammunition and went with us. Our company was ordered to support the rapid firing guns and so again we were left in the rear. But my how the bullets did come over and near us. Treen was willing to take his place with us down behind a rice ridge. I believe he would make a good "scrapper." He sends his regards.

Say I see by the paper that the people at home are "kicking" about Col. Stotsenburg. I believe that most of the trouble is at home. The Col has made this regiment what it is and it is a good one, about one of the best Vol. reg. here. We had hard drills while at Camp Santa Mesa but not at all more than we needed since we have got into this trouble. I notice that those who did not attend these drills are now all worn out. We have a great deal of ground to cover now and if it had not been for the gradual bringing up to this hard work we would not be in it.

The Neb Boys, with four guns handled by the brave steady hands of the Utah [artillery] battery, see some scrapping – well it averages nearly every other day.

Co E is at the Reservoir. Co. G near there and Co. B between it and the reservoir, and Co. H between the reservoir and the Water Works. These companies make up the 3rd Battalion. The other battalions are at or near the water works and the Utah boys, except Co. C which is at Camp Santa Mesa. Their officer being wounded. It is 4 or 5 miles between the Water Works and the Reservoir. Now from that you can see what Neb. & the Utah battery holds down. The dark devils being on both sides and east end.

Well I must stop but not 'til I say a little more.

Col. Stotsenburg, the paper said, ordered sick men's names taken off the sick report just before reports were sent in. The Col may have gone a little too far there but not meaningly. You know as well as I do that there are some men who will slough around and get on the sick book by their own "gall" or carelessness and let others do their work. These men should have their names scratched off the sick book.

It is just these men – "Sore Heads" who write home troubles they cause themselves or imagine.

Of course the Colonel is a regular officer and very strict, but that is what brought our regiment to the front.

Run

Marginal note – You don't need to worry. I'll keep that empty "nut" [head] of mine ducked.

On the Offensive

In mid-March the Nebraska volunteers were relieved from their assignment guarding the waterworks and pipeline. They exchanged positions with the First Colorado troops then moved down the pipeline for a short but well deserved rest near Block House 5.

Courtesy of Nebraska State Historical Society

Company E Camped at Pumping Station.

The Filipino troops, having been pushed out of their strong position on the Santa Mesa Ridge, reformed at Caloocan. They were twelve miles from Manila on the extreme left end of the American line. With the American troops pressing hard, the Filipinos continued their retreat and the Americans captured Caloocan, an important railroad center.

Included in the Caloocan "take" were five locomotives, fifty passenger coaches, and a hundred freight cars. The rolling stock was rapidly repaired and put into service for the Army. One train was loaded up to follow the troops as a supply train

Nina Hull Miller Collection

Captured Train at Caloocan.

Over the next few days a locomotive and several cars were outfitted as an armored train with heavy steel plating surrounding a six-pound cannon, a Hotchkiss rotating cannon, and two or three machine guns.

Courtesy National Museum of the Marine Corps

Hotchkiss Rotating Cannon.

On March 25th a major offensive campaign was launched to pursue the Filipino Army and to capture Malolos, Aguinaldo's capital about twenty miles north of Manila. The Nebraskans left their defensive position near the block houses and moved northeast to the village of San Fernando del Monte. There, stiff resistance was encountered, with hand-to-hand fighting, the first for the Nebraskans.

156

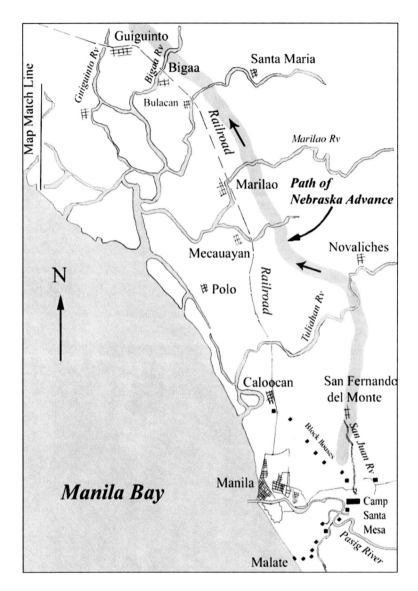

The 1st Nebraska's Advance North Through Marilao.

Continuing past San Fernando del Monte the first objective was the town of Novaliches, but thick jungle and bogs made advances in that direction near impossible. The troops neared the Tuliahan River but were well short of the town and they were exhausted. With further advances nearly impossible, tactical orders soon changed. The Nebraskans were redirected to cross the Tuliahan River and advance toward Mecauayan, moving along their lengthy right flank. Enemy detachments, skillful in using the jungle to advantage, fought an effective delaying action. As the temperature soared, numerous soldiers were overcome by sunstroke. Many discarded anything heavy - their bayonets, haversacks, ponchos, and even food.

Courtesy of Nebraska State Historical Society

Troopers Resting.

At the Tuliahan River the approach was narrow and the nearby bridge heavily defended. However, a small detachment of troopers slipped across the river upstream of the bridge, then attacked from the Filipino's flank and broke their defense. The successful crossing of the Tuliahan River was crucial and prevented an ambush of the division's supply train as it followed the advancing troops.

Along the advance, Filipinos contested every stream and open-field crossing. Americans were spread out on both sides of the railroad, over eight miles without any coordinated action. As the volunteers approached the Mecauayan River the Filipinos put up a fierce fight and in the ensuing bloody battle more than 90 Filipino soldiers were killed.

On the following day American troops pressed doggedly on and reached the Marilao River. Crossing here was tougher. They faced a river over 200 feet wide with a damaged and heavily defended railroad bridge. The troops stopped, reluctant to cross. There was no deck. The ties were 2½ feet apart and the bridge was high. The soldiers paused, concerned about being under fire and falling from the bridge with all their equipment.

As they hesitated, five volunteers swam across the river upstream, seized a bamboo raft, and pushed it back to the south shore. With the raft carrying 22 volunteers and their equipment, they re-crossed the river and attacked the Filipino troops from the rear. At the same time some of the waiting troops were led across the bridge with bullets ricocheting off the bridge steel around them. Other troops waded across.

Courtesy of Nebraska State Historical Society

Company G Wading Across the Marilao River.

Later in afternoon the Filipinos counter-attacked. By this time the entire regiment had now crossed the bridge. They charged the Filipinos, routed them, and chased them for two miles. General Hale exclaimed, "There go those Nebraskans, and all hell couldn't stop them!"

Nebraskans remained at Marilao for two days to help to repair the railroad bridge. On March 29th the 1st Nebraska moved up the railroad line past Santa Maria, Santa Clara, across the Bigaa River, past Bigaa, Bulacan, and Guiguinto. Often they advanced under heavy fire. The following day, after crossing the Guiguinto River, the troops paused to distribute ammunition and rations, then resumed the advance two more miles under continuing heavy fire.

As one of the soldiers wrote home:[53]

"We were behind the firing line about 300 yards marching in column of fours. ... The officers didn't have to tell the boys to keep their heads down. The minute [the firing] opened up every man dropped. He didn't have to be told. ... It was a sad sight to look at when we got up to where the firing line was. Twenty-three of our boys were scattered along the line."

The Kansas Regiment was the first to enter Malolos. They found the town empty and buildings on all sides were bursting into flames. As they had left, Filipino General Luna's forces had ignited the town to deny its use by their enemy. When the fires burned themselves out, nothing but charred houses remained.[54] Aguinaldo's government had withdrawn to San Isidro thirty miles farther up the railroad line.

---

[53] Thiessen, p. 251.
[54] Linn, p. 99.

Courtesy of Nebraska State Historical Society

Nebraska Troopers Resting Along the Railroad.

Since the beginning of the Malolos offensive 1st Nebraska suffered greatly: 65 killed, 478 wounded. The troops were completely worn out and only one-third of the regiment was fit for duty when they reached Malolos.

In a letter written by Hull's hometown neighbor Luther Abbot, he describes the town:

"The street along which our division is camped has been all appropriated by the soldiers. Houses are occupied by officers and men, many have been dismantled, all have been looted. The natives made a great mistake in not letting their women return, also non-combatants, as soon as the fighting was over. Then they would have had a home. Now, they have nothing. The reason they did not come back was probably because we were painted as devils. Our only hope of peace is to convince them by our conduct we are not. This is the only way of conquering the Philippines in my opinion."

The Malolos campaign highlighted a significant problem that had been known from the outset. The volunteers were armed with single-shot Springfield rifles. The Regular Infantry were armed with the newer Norwegian Krag-Jorgensen rifles.

Nina Hull Miller Collection

Smoke From Obsolete Springfield Rifles.

The Springfield rifles were clearly inadequate.[55] The Springfield weapon took a long time to reload. It was heavy, "kicked like a mule," and was woefully inaccurate at long range. The dense white clouds from the cartridge's black powder were easily spotted and earned the rifle the nickname "Smoke Wagon." To improve the weapon the War Department issued smokeless ammunition, but those cartridges split the Springfield's barrels and blew out the breech blocks.

Many of the Filipinos were equipped with Mauser rifles, with much greater range. Against those rifles the volunteers were at a serious disadvantage unless they were backed up by artillery or Regular Army troops armed with more modern "Krags." The "Krags" had a five-shot magazine and used smokeless powder.

Krag-Jorgenson

The rifle "problem" existed apparently because Commanding General Otis was needlessly stingy with equipment. Early in November he requested 8,000 "Krags," but then ordered only 3,000 shipped to Manila. Not until the following April did he request more, and then only another 3,000.

---

55 Linn, p. 100.

10. *The Push to San Fernando*

As American troops captured Malolos the Filipinos were still fighting, effectively blocking the American effort to press northward and capture their leadership and temporary capital.

Courtesy of Nebraska State Historical Society

Regimental Headquarters at Malolos.

165

Once in Malolos the Nebraska Volunteers camped there for more than three weeks, partially recovering from their exhausting advance through the jungle and across the countless streams. The troops were unaware that even more challenging terrain was ahead.

Meanwhile, General Luna's Filipino army made the most of the pause. They busily dug entrenchments behind the several rivers north of Malolos and prepared to blow up both roadway and railway bridges in the path of the American troops.

Courtesy of Nebraska State Historical Society

Malolos, with Soldiers Camped in the Plaza.

Manila, Apr, 8 '99

Dear People,

I started to write yesterday in a box car at Malolos but I had to stop and come to Manila with another car. You see about a month ago we came in from the Water-Works and changed places with the Colo. for a rest! Well while we were there in our new position, near block house 5. ... Our officer being canteen officer[56] started a branch canteen there and put me in charge. We got nearly 2 weeks of rest and had the canteen there about 3 or 4 days when orders came to pack up everything and get ready to move. I got the branch over to the main canteen in time to go with the company and there I have been except for the last few days.

When we got to Malolos, Cap. sent me back after the canteen and we have been running railroad cars of canned goods for that place since. It doesn't take long to empty a car or two.

Our regiment was in it from start to finish and being on the extreme right we got the hardest part. This first day in Malolos only 460 reported for duty. The rest are wounded or sick in the hospital.

---

[56] The officer responsible for the food supplies.

> *We have had 13 wounded in our company, no one very bad. One wounded in my squad.*
>
> *25 out of each company were given new guns. Soon all will have them and the Springfields will be quiet.*
>
> *Well I must stop. I will write more soon. I think we stay at Malolos.*
>
> *Run*

Two days after Runnie's letter, General Luna's Filipino troops attacked several locations along the railroad. To drive back the insurgents the American troops started back down the railroad toward Marilao. At Guiguinto they discovered a strong enemy force had effectively hidden in the nearby jungle and were pouring heavy fire into the American ranks. The Americans brought up their recently armored train and pushed it along the railroad, where the newly mounted cannon and machine guns effectively tore into the hidden attackers.

The American offensive was planned to start April 24th but fighting was inadvertently started a day early. A scouting party from the Nebraska Regiment moved to reconnoiter in the vicinity of Quingua, were surprised by heavy Filipino fire from the nearby bamboo thickets, and were pinned down in a ditch.

Major Frank Eager, who was roundly criticized later, led four companies of Nebraskans to relieve the beleaguered men, but the rescuers were led into the same devastating fire from the Filipinos and were also pinned down. Both the American scouts and would-be rescuers were unable to either advance or pull back. They were caught in an open field and an exposed position. There they sweltered for two hours under oppressive tropical heat.

Another battalion of Nebraskans and a battalion of Iowans arrived and were poised to advance, but they were hesitant to do so in the face of withering fire. Colonel Stotsenburg, just returning from Manila, saw no other way to extricate his men and immediately led all eight companies in a charge, firing as they went. Colonel Stotsenburg, out in front, was fatally hit, but his men continued their advance with great determination, routing the Filipinos from their positions. Major Bell, who was leading one of the rescue companies, reported, "He placed himself in front of the regiment and with hat in one hand and pistol in the other led it against the trenches of the insurgents, routing them completely."

Runnie described the encounter in a letter written from San Fernando two weeks later and lamented the loss of his leader: "The death of the Colonel in particular went hard. ... We all loved and respected him." In Runnie's next letter he would again catch up on reports of his activities. This time the chronology was more frightening. The following is from his letter of May 19th:

May 19

Dear Folks

The last time I wrote we were in Malolos. Now we are about 5 miles beyond. I was working in the canteen business as I wrote before and was ordered to report to the company on Apr 24 when a general advance was to be made. But the trouble started Sunday morning April 23. The Cavalry had started out early on a scouting trip and were attacked between Malolos and Quingua. Maj. Eager took his Bat. out there and had them out there in the hot sun 2 or 3 hours close to the rice ridges as they could get, bullets flying close all of the time.

Our Colonel was in Manila. He heard about it as he got off the train at Malolos and grabbed his revolver and started out. The boys said that the Col said Eager had placed his men in a death trap. And everyone says that Eager's mis-management caused this scrap (which was meant for the whole brigade the next day) and the loss of 40 men killed and wounded and our Colonel.

I hope someday the army will be made up of men that can have something to say about their officers without being liable to be court marshaled and shot and of officers that know their business and not just put in their own account of their political foolishness.

I have heard men say that if Eager ever became Col, they would refuse to act.

This is what I hear from others. I have nothing to say myself. The blue book forbids it. ...

Nina Hull Miller Collection

Runnie Resting at Malolos.

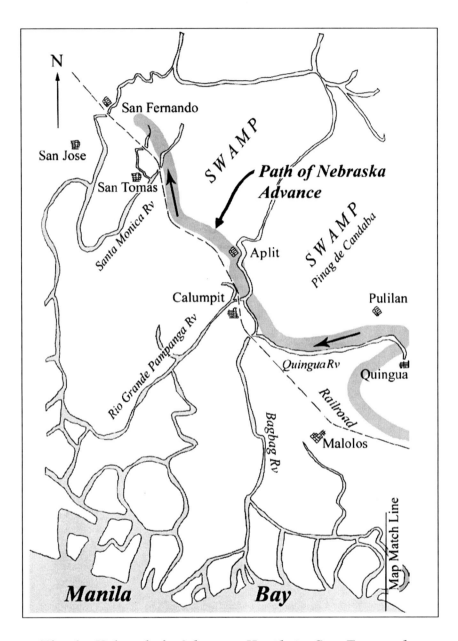

The 1ˢᵗ Nebraska's Advance North to San Fernando.

The planned offensive got underway April 24th. After artillery pounded trenches across the Quingua River, the 1st Nebraskans fought their way across the bridge and then advanced along the river toward Calumpit.

Luther Abbot[57] wrote about the miserable conditions:

"The insurgents were entrenched in Quingua about 600 yards from our firing line. ... We advanced double time under heavy fire. The sun was as bad as the bullets. Finally within 50 yards of the firing line we lay down and waited. It was sweltering. We were compelled to keep close behind the rice ridge and the steam from the wet ground of the rain the night before fairly boiled our faces. There was no breeze. While laying here Peters of our squad had a sun stroke and went into fits. ... The heat was something awful. But I ran for the timber. The rebels saw me plainly and the bullets zipped and sang all about me....

"The battalion in reserve came up and a vicious fire opened up. We lay down thinking we had better stay put until the line advanced more. This it did by rushes. ... The line kept going forward. First one company and then another would

---

[57] Luther Abbot was a neighbor from their hometown of Fremont, Nebraska.

rush. As the line approached the rebel works, the fire grew even hotter...."

The Nebraska and South Dakota regiments, in three successive engagements, drove the Filipinos about two miles west of Pulilan. Here the brigade bivouacked.

The next day the offensive resumed with the troops advancing along the railroad line. The objective was the town of Calumpit on the Rio Grande de Pampanga.

About a mile south of Calumpit the Quingua River merges into the Bagbag River. About a mile upstream the Calumpit River connects the Rio Grande de Pampanga and Bagbag-Quingua Rivers. Near this major river confluence are two important railroad bridges, and here the Filipinos set up a strong defense. Several thousand insurgents were entrenched along both rivers, presenting a formidable obstacle to the American advance.

As the Nebraska Regiment approached the Calumpit River from the east, the First Brigade arrived at the south bank of the Bagbag to find the railroad bridge had been destroyed.

Both brigades opened artillery fire on the enemy trenches and then followed up to within range of their Springfield rifles. First Nebraska crossed the rivers successfully, routed the Filipinos, and swept northward through the town of Calumpit.

Courtesy of Nebraska State Historical Society

The Calumpit River Bridge Destroyed By the Retreating Filipino Troops.

The next railroad bridge, crossing the Rio Grande de Pampanga, was not so easily taken. It was strongly fortified by Filipino positions which had to be cleared before the advance could continue. The American troops were stalled. Individually the Filipinos fought bravely, but their troops suffered from lack of strong leadership. After being pounded by the artillery, the bridge defenses finally withered in the face of the better disciplined Americans.

One of Runnie's Letters Home.

The following excerpt from Runnie's letter of May 9th describes the offensive:

...Sunday evening the brigade formed at Quingua, the place taken when Col. Stotsenburg was killed. The next morning, after the cannon had poured in plenty of metal we, Neb., So. Dak., & Iowa moved with the battery from across the river and started out in a long line toward Calumpit. The Iowa's right reached to the swamp of Candaba and Neb's left on the river with So. Dakota in the center. It took two days to get to their works on the Rio Bagbag.

The RR bridge is broken here so we stayed at this place a number of days while Wheaton's brigade who had joined us there moved forward to the Calumpit about 2 miles beyond.

Three days ago we started for San Fernando and here we are. And it is dinner time now so I will stop. Tell my friends that I'm well.

Run

On May 4th after driving the Filipino forces from the town of Apalit, the Nebraska troops advanced along the railroad escorting a supply train. They passed water holes polluted by corpses thrown in by the retreating troops and discovered Filipinos setting up an insidious defense line. The retreating troops dug numerous deep pits and spiked the bottom with sharpened bamboo, then camouflaged them with the "normal" jungle litter. The pits were a surprise, but once spotted became less difficult to avoid.

The advancing Nebraskans were then sent around the Filipinos' defenses through the swampland and jungle muck east of the railroad. As they reached Santo Tomas the troops were exhausted and unable to call up any reserve strength to go farther.

Meanwhile, the Kansas and Iowa troops pressed forward along the railroad and captured San Fernando and a cache of 100 rifles. After a night's rest, the Nebraskans struggled into San Fernando to join the rest of the troops.

Although the General wanted to press on, all of the troops were exhausted. The troops had advanced more than 40 miles, much of it through jungle or swamp, and under fire. Only half the Volunteer troops were fit for duty. In particular, the condition of the 1st Nebraska Regiment was extreme: 35 killed, 151 wounded, 36 discharged for disability, 281 in hospital, and 125 sick in quarters. And the doctors announced they would not send anyone to the hospital unless they were so sick they could not walk. The regiment of 923 men now had less than 300 men fit for duty.[58]

The Nebraskans entered San Fernando on May 6th. Although other troops carried the offensive forward, the Nebraska Regiment remained to occupy San Fernando until May 20th when they were relieved of front-line duty. The troops then marched several miles to Calumpit where they boarded a train for Manila and "cheered themselves hoarse."

In Manila, the Nebraskans augmented the Provost Guard units to provide security in and about the city. The men were detailed to guard duty at various key locations and were thankful for the comparatively uneventful "recovery" time.

---

[58] Thiessen, p. 255.

Homeward Bound

The insurgents, however, had not given up. Far from it. By the end of May, the Filipino forces were staging relentless hit-and-run operations not only at San Fernando but along the entire tenuously held 40-mile railroad corridor.

Malate, June 5, 1899

Dear sister Nina,[59]

I think this is about time I was writing to you, don't you? We live in Malate now and very nearly by the bay where big waves come tumbling in on the sand. Get Mama to show you on the map.

Nina, shall I tell you how we do when we fight?

While we were at the water works, if the Filipinos came too close we would get up early in the morning before they could see us and go after them. We would go slow 'til they began to shoot, then we would run at them and when we got very close to them the officers would tell us to shoot. Soon you could see a Filipino get up and run then another and another and when we yelled and shot and then gave a big yell they run faster. The whole big lot of them

---

[59] Nina, his youngest sister was seven-years-old at the time.

would scatter and run like a big family of small chickens and we wouldn't let them stop for an hour.

When we went to Malolos we had to drive them from behind big banks of dirt. Some time there were so many behind these banks that we would have to run a ways then drop down behind rice ridges for a while so we would not get hit by their bullets and then a little farther shooting all the time.

When we got up close and yelled and charged on them you should have been there to see them run.

I will send some pictures home in a bamboo joint. Tell me if you get them. "Doc" Abbot[60] says tell Nina Hello and to give his regards to the others. I sent Clyde some fun sketches. Did he get them?

Run

The way a Chinaman writes 'run' is this

---

[60] "Doc" is Luther Abbot, Runnie's Fremont neighbor.

Back home in America there was a serious and growing situation. The volunteers' year of enlistment was ending. Troops were asking when?

And there was increasing civilian pressure for them to return home. They were proud, but increasingly questioning the basis for the American presence there.

The pending departure from the Philippines of 16,000 volunteers was to be offset by 7,000 Regular Army troops. The situation caused a substantial rethinking on the part of the generals. Finally on June 21st recall orders were received by the volunteers and the troops boarded the SS *Hancock* for the voyage back to the states.

The SS *Hancock* first stopped at Nagasaki, Japan to take on coal. There were additional stops in Tokyo Bay and then at Yokohama. Most of the troops took full advantage of these stops for sightseeing and buying souvenirs. Runnie bought a kimono, and other special items, to take home for his sisters, but he and the rest of the troops were more than ready when the ship finally left July 15, 1899 for the States.

Courtesy of Nebraska State Historical Society

The SS *Hancock* with Troops Ready to Disembark.

Courtesy of Nebraska State Historical Society

The Welcome in San Francisco.

When the SS *Hancock* arrived in San Francisco July 29th the men were quarantined until the stateside doctors could check them over. When they finally docked at Pier 12 a wildly celebrating public engulfed the ship and the troops as they marched to a new tent camp in the Presidio (not at the dismal Camp Merritt which the volunteers had occupied a year earlier).

Courtesy of Presidio Trust Library

Tent Camp at the San Francisco Presidio to Temporarily House the Returning Troops.

Arundel Miller Hull Collection

Company H in San Francisco Awaiting Discharge.

Arundel Miller Hull Collection

**Recreation for the Returning Troops
at San Francisco's Sutro Baths.**

The volunteers cooled their heels at the Presidio for nearly a month, providing time for the troop's physical condition to improve and paperwork to catch up. Finally, on August 23rd the Nebraska volunteers were officially mustered out and boarded special trains for home.

When the Nebraska Volunteer Regiment returned the unit consisted of 45 officers and 842 enlisted men.

At the peak of the Philippine-American conflict 126,000 U.S. soldiers were needed to occupy and pacify the islands. By the war's end, 1902, more than 4,200 U.S. soldiers and 20,000 Filipino soldiers were dead, along with 200,000 Filipino civilians.

San Francisco, August 1899

Dear Folks,

I suppose you "sabe" that I am a poor fellow to write letters. I knew that you knew that we were at "Frisco" as soon or sooner than we knew it so I didn't worry any about that.

I got the Breast Protector[61] all right and the papers and letters.

I've been well all of the time. I spend most of the day in the dining room writing out the muster rolls. Mr. T. Frahn lives just 6 blocks from here and "Doc" and I have been to his house a number of evenings. He always tells me how "dad" used to go and see him when he was sick. I always have a good time there and lots to eat.

Of course you know we are to be mustered out Aug 23rd, but I don't know when we start for home.

When I get home I'm going to the YMCA and take a bath before I go home so it won't do you any good for any of you to be at the depot. ...

If I don't write any more you don't need to worry.

Run

---

[61] The breast protector was a strip of flannel which contained camphor or eucalyptus, worn across the chest and thought to ward off fever.

GREETS A FREMONT BOY

City Welcomes Runnie Hull of the Fighting First

OVATION GIVEN AT THE DEPOT

Cheered by the Crowd as He Stepped Off the Car — Cannon Booms Out the Tidings --- Escort Awaits Him on the Platform --- Clarence Fay and Charley Kelly not yet in the City

Runnie Hull returned home this afternoon after having served with the fighting First Nebraska in the Philippines. On coming with the regiment from the coast he stopped over with his comrades of Company H, at Nelson, and was present for their reception.

Fremonters have been on the alert to hear of the return of any of the boys who went to Manila from Fremont and when it became known that the Superior train would bring one of the heroes back home news spread quickly. There was a large crowd of citizens at the station to catch the first glimpse of the soldier. Members of the Grand Army of the Republic, the Sons of Veterans and soldiers of the Second and Third Nebraska Regiments were on hand and Jake May's cannon was primed in readiness. As the train pulled in a cheer rose from the crowd, the cannon boomed out and Runnie Hull, bronzed from the effects of the campaign in the tropics, stepped off the train. Clad in his khaki uniform he did not look much altered since he went away with his regiment. The members of the family greeted him as he got off the train and his friends crowded around him to grasp his hand. A huge wreath of flowers was thrown over his head and he was escorted from the station to his home by rejoicing friends. The band struck up a lively air for Runnie and the crowd on the platform.

Fremont Tribune, August 30, 1899

By late summer 1899 most of the volunteer troops returned to the U. S. leaving the Regular Army to occupy and pacify the Islands.

The Philippine war was far from over, however. The Filipino leader was moving throughout Luzon, regrouping the insurgents, making bold guerilla raids, and eluding the Americans. Finally in 1901, in a daring operation, a Kansas Volunteer officer, Fredrick Funston, led a group of disguised "captives" into Aguinaldo's headquarters where they overpowered him along with a small contingent of his followers.

In 1902, the U.S. Congress passed legislation establishing the first elected Philippine government. Sporadic guerrilla encounters continued even longer on Luzon and other islands in the archipelago. Full Filipino independence did not come, however, until 1946, after the end of both World Wars I and II.

11. And At Home

The returning soldiers were at a distinct disadvantage. Many were sick or injured when discharged, and most were at loose ends. Runnie was among the fortunate few. He was apparently the only volunteer from his hometown, and on his return the townspeople greeted him with enthusiasm and appreciation.

His parents were particularly proud. Even more so were his sisters May, Bessie, and Nina, for when Runnie's ship had stopped in Japan he had gathered up souvenirs for each of them.

Nina Hull Miller Collection
Sisters May, Nina, Bessie.

Nina Hull Miller Collection
Bessie in a Souvenir Kimono.

After resting at home in Fremont, Arundel Miller Hull returned to the University of Nebraska, where he continued his studies in electrical engineering. He became a member of the Pershing Rifles drill team and with his experience in actual combat was appointed Cadet Major of the R.O.T.C. Battalion. In 1903 he graduated with a degree in Electrical Engineering.

Nina Hull Miller Collection

**Arundel Miller Hull
as the R.O.T.C. Cadet Major.**

After graduation, Runnie worked in various mid-west towns installing municipal electric power plants. One of the plants was in Wisner, Nebraska where he encountered Adelaide Deily, whom he had previously met at the University. Romance blossomed and in September 1906 he brought her home to Fremont for an introductory visit. In October they married and soon they were off to power plant jobs in northern Colorado and at Carthage, Missouri.

Their two boys, Arundel Deily Hull and Henry Elwin Hull, were born in 1907 and 1909.

In 1911, Runnie became ill with pneumonia. He and his family returned to Wisner where he succumbed. Runnie was buried in the Hull family plot in Fremont. His family, Adelaide and the two boys, continued as a close part of the Hull family for many years.

PART III 1919
Glenn: A French *Croix de Guerre*

Glenn Eugene Miller

<u>Glenn Eugene Miller</u>

Born: May 28, 1894
1916   University of Nebraska, B.A. / R.O.T.C.
1916-1917 High School Principal,
           Beaver City, Nebraska
1917-1919 U. S. Army, Fort Snelling, Minnesota,
           Fort Harrison, Indiana, Camp Bowie, Texas,
           A.E.F. France, Meuse-Argonne,
           Awarded French *Croix de Guerre*
1921   Married Nina Hull
1921-1934 Principal, then Superintendent of
           Schools, Ravenna, Nebraska
1929   University of Nebraska, M.A.
1935-1956 Superintendent of Schools,
           Lexington, Nebraska
1957-1959 Right-of-Way Appraiser, Nebraska State
           Highway Department
1963-1964 Dawson County Judge
1966-1970 Lexington City Council
Died: July 25, 1982

12. European Turmoil

The early 1900s emerged as a period of churning political turmoil in Europe. Disputes over territory and distrust between ethnic groups and neighboring countries led to a complex fabric of treaties and overlapping agreements for mutual defense. As frequently occurs, an unlikely event in June 1914 triggered a chain of momentous events.

In 1914 Archduke Franz Ferdinand, heir to the Austro-Hungarian throne, made a trip to Sarajevo, the capital of Bosnia-Herzegovina, to head off a movement in Bosnia to become part of the independent Slav nation of Serbia. Despite various conciliatory efforts, members of the revolutionary movement remained committed to Bosnian independence. Four of the zealous insurgents collected arms and positioned themselves along the Archduke's travel route. One of the insurgents tossed a bomb at the Archduke's car. The bomb bounced off the car before it exploded, but as the driver turned around to take a safer route, he stopped momentarily directly in front of the second insurgent. The zealot fired his revolver at point blank range, killing both the Archduke and his wife.

Ethnic rivalry exploded! The Austrians, eager to expand their influence, saw the assassination as an opportunity to invade Serbia, but they needed a better reason before they could "legitimately" make their move. The Austrians made a series of ten rather extreme demands of the Serbs . . . to be met or agreed to within 48 hours. Surprisingly, the Serbs agreed to all but one. However, Austria wouldn't let the matter be settled and impulsively declared war. The fabric of agreements between European countries began to unravel. Serbia had been promised support by Czar Nicolas, who mobilized thirteen Russian Army corps as a warning to Austria. The German Kaiser, bound by a pledge to Austria, demanded that the Russians demobilize. The bombastic and overbearing Kaiser Wilhelm was contemptuous of everyone and eager to prove his toughness, especially to Great Britain. He demanded that Russia demobilize within 12 hours or Germany would declare war.

The Germans, however, were now faced with a quandary: France had an alliance with Russia. If Germans entered the fray, France, allied with Russia, could not remain neutral. Thus Germany was faced with the prospect of a two-front war, the Russians on the east and France on the west. Judging that the Russian move would be ponderously slow, the Germans chose to attack France, expecting to neutralize it before turning toward Russia. To avoid the heavily defended French border, the Germans planned to roll into France through Belgium.

Now Britain, which thought it was well removed from the Balkan quarrel, was faced with the prospect of German forces a scant few miles across the English Channel and they were treaty-bound for the defense of Belgium. Even though the British had no great interest in helping France, there was no way for them to avoid it.

Das Pickelhaube
(German Military Helmet)

War was declared and in a matter of a few weeks all of Europe was embroiled in the conflict. Germany, Austria-Hungary, and the Ottoman Empire (the "Central Powers") were now arrayed worldwide against the "Entente Powers": Russia, France, and Britain, and later Italy and the United States. The military planners in Germany, France, and Russia all based their plans on offensive strikes and depended on speed to gain their victory. Once their plans were set in motion, poor communications and diplomatic impotence made it impossible for any of them to turn back.

Europe 1914.

13. American Entry

At the outset of the European squabble the United States was staunchly isolationist. However, in 1915 a German submarine torpedoed and sank the British passenger liner, *Lusitania,* only 14 miles from the Irish shore. There were 128 Americans aboard. With this direct threat to American lives, the attitude of the American public began to change. President Woodrow Wilson tried unsuccessfully to negotiate a settlement between the Entente and Central Powers.

Meanwhile, former President Teddy Roosevelt loudly "rattled the saber" and called the sinking an act of piracy. An intercepted and decoded German message further fueled the public outrage. The Germans had asked the Mexican government to join in the fight and even suggested they try to induce Japan as well. The Germans promised they would support the Mexican government in its effort to reclaim Texas, New Mexico, and Arizona. The American public soon abandoned its isolationism and clamored for retaliation.

In Europe, the German invasion of Belgium and France lost its momentum as troops from throughout the British Commonwealth entered the fray. Neither side was able to gain a decisive advantage along the 475 mile Western Front. And as the war dragged along, France and England were soon stretched economically. To raise money the British sold their interests in the American railroads and both governments borrowed heavily from American lenders. If the Allies went under, many U.S. firms would also be bankrupt. It was soon obvious that U.S. neutrality was no longer an option and that American interests lay with the Entente Powers.

When German submarines cut deeply into the ocean shipping across the Atlantic and threatened the east coast of the United States President Woodrow Wilson reluctantly sought Congressional approval to join the Entente nations as an "Associated Power." On April 6, 1917, the United States declared war.

However, the U.S. was in no condition to fight. There were only 107,000 poorly trained men in the Army and 122,000 men in the National Guard, half of whom had never fired a rifle. The Army soon organized for rapid growth around existing National Guard units from each state, and in mid-July a national draft law was enacted. Initial recruitment was fueled by individual patriotism, but soon four million draftees had been added. Each soldier was outfitted with uniforms costing $156.30, and a $19.50 rifle.

President Wilson reached way down in the seniority list of Army generals and picked "Black Jack" Pershing to head the American Expeditionary Force to France, the "A.E.F." Pershing acquired the moniker from his former command of black troops during the earlier U.S. "police action" along the Mexican border. Part of his new challenge was to deal effectively with the British and French generals.

Glenn E. Miller Collection
U.S. Troops Crossing the Atlantic.

By the summer of 1918, Army units with fresh soldiers loaded onto troopships, crossed the submarine infested Atlantic, and landed in French ports nearly every day.

But "fresh" was hardly an accurate way to describe the troops. Several passenger ships had been converted to troop carriers. The somewhat spacious accommodations for civilian passengers were now housing as many as 6,000 soldiers along with their personal gear. Men were crammed into every space. There was no room to sit or even stand. Occasionally, some of the troops were allowed to come on deck. Otherwise, the only place to "be" was in airless compartments where the bunks were six-high, the toilets clogged, and the results of seasickness was prevalent everywhere.

After the ships left the proximity of the American shore, periodic "abandon-ship" drills kept everyone on edge, standing at the rails ready to jump into the inky blackness. The existence of only 20 life boats and 20-30 rafts was hardly reassuring to the hundreds of men aboard.

Glenn E. Miller Collection
USS *Pueblo*, One of Many Troopships.

14. R. O. T. C.

The R.O.T.C., Reserve Officer Training Corps, was established in colleges which had received federal land grants for their campuses. The program required male freshmen and sophomores to undergo introductory military training. Junior and senior students could opt for additional training and receive a stipend during their last two years, but only with a commitment for a period of active Army duty.

For a young man from a small town in Nebraska the University and the R. O. T. C. offered a venture into a bigger world. For Glenn Miller his four years of University and R. O. T. C. culminated in June of 1916 with a B.A. degree and 2nd Lieutenant's bars. Following his graduation he was hired as Principal of the Beaver City, Nebraska, High School, but his "teaching" career was soon to take a pause.

2nd Lt. Glenn E. Miller.

When the United States entered the European conflict Glenn was counted among many young men eager to join in. By August 1917 he received orders to active duty in the 2nd Reserve Officer Training Corps at Fort Snelling, Minnesota. Here, weather was disagreeably similar to northern Europe – rainy and cold. Training fields were designed to give realistic training for those young Americans who were about to be thrown into the fray.

Glenn E. Miller Collection

Fort Snelling Barracks.

The Training Fields

The training fields represented the military thinking of the time. Artillery had advanced since the Civil and Spanish-American Wars to become much more powerful and accurate. Defenses were driven below ground: dugouts, interlaced trenches, cratered mud holes, and fields of barbed wire. The hand-dug trenches extended along three irregular lines spaced several hundred yards apart. The very front line was the fire-line trench, second back was the support trench, and farther back yet a reserve trench. The front-line trench had short sections jutting out front – "saps"- for observation and to create positions for crossfire on attacking troops.

Glenn E. Miller Collection
Rifle Range at Fort Snelling.

Glenn E. Miller Collection
Training Trenches at Fort Snelling.

Glenn E. Miller Collection
More Training Trenches at Fort Snelling.

Perpendicular trenches connected the three rows. All three lines then turned every few yards to limit line of fire and limit the effects of shrapnel from exploding artillery. Barbed wire and sandbags were everywhere. On the front side of the trenches was some kind of dirt step or sandbags to allow men to step up to fire and hurl grenades. Trench sides were shored up with sandbags, corrugated iron, or willow branches.

At the end of an intensive three months training at Fort Snelling, Glenn was commissioned a 1st Lieutenant and shipped off to Fort Benjamin Harrison in Indiana.

15. Stateside Training

For the first few weeks at Fort Benjamin Harrison Glenn was among the numerous fresh Lieutenants waiting for reassignment. Some were destined for existing understaffed regiments or newly organized units. They encountered the Army mantra of "hurry up and wait." Glenn's letters home related his varied new experiences as a soldier, but mainly reflected his boredom.

Letter 2-19-1918

> Fort Benjamin Harrison, Indiana
>
> Dear Folks,
>
> I was on guard again last Sunday. This will be a regular occurrence in the future for the Company will go on guard every six days from now on. As we have a surplus of officers on hand. I will catch it about every third time. As usual nothing very exciting happened, except a few of the boys caught a few vermin and we soon fixed them by fumigating their clothes.
>
> Your loving son, Glenn

Letter 3-22-1918

Fort Benjamin Harrison, Indiana

Dear Folks,

The 10th seems to be on the duty roster for guard duty. And another Company leaves tonight to guard a bridge somewhere in West Virginia. ...That leaves six companies here at the post. So we go on guard every four days and Glenn goes on tonight at 5 pm as Officer of the Day. We hear various rumors as to what will become of us and it is certain that something will happen soon for we have eleven or twelve officers with each company doing the work of three. And my guess is that either more troops will be sent to this post or else we will be moved to a National Army Camp somewhere. So in the mean time we are preparing ourselves the best we can.

Your loving son Glenn

Letter 3-31-1918

Fort Benjamin Harrison, Indiana

Dear Folks,

The big drive has not affected us in the least except that we seem to be the dumping ground for all the unfit. Last night we received a number of aliens and mental unfits from the National Army. So this leads one to believe that the 10th [Infantry] will do guard duty. ... Say, you certainly had a proud son Friday afternoon, the Company Commander left for town early and Glenn had command of the Company at Battalion Parade and when he marched in front of the Company past the reviewing officers his stock was selling at way above par. This in itself is not such a big stunt but I happened to be the first Reserve officer to pull it. Our Company Commander is also Judge Advocate and so Glenn has had virtual command of the Company during the periods of drill and instruction. ... The opinion at the present time is that we will soon receive a large number of drafted men ... and then our work will begin.

Your loving son Glenn

During the previous year when Glenn was Principal at Beaver City, he became friends with the teachers there. When he left for the Army one of them, Miss Martha Goehry, struck up a correspondence with him and sent him a "Soldier's Diary." He dutifully made daily entries until August 31, 1918 when it was filled.

Diary 6-14-1918

Fort Benjamin Harrison, Indiana

Made second in command of Co. L 10th Infantry and finished the range. Score, 263/400. Looks small but will average well.

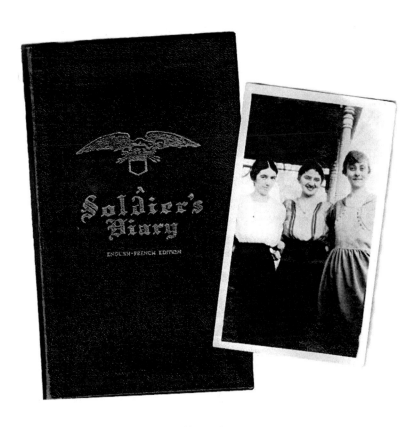

Teachers:
Misses Flanders, Goehry, and McKenney.

Organizing the 36th Division

Later in June, Glenn was transferred from Fort Benjamin Harrison to Camp McArthur in Texas. There the Army was forming the 36th Division. Even with National Guard units from both Oklahoma and Texas the division was considerably under strength. To fill it out they assigned newly-arrived Lieutenants and many recent recruits and draftees just out of basic training.

Letter 6-20-1918

Mailed from El Paso, Texas,

Dear Folks,

Well here goes. Left Indianapolis at noon yesterday. ... Am now just out of Marshall Texas where it is so dam hot that Negros carry umbrellas at 9 in the morning. The country I have seen this morning is mostly wooded, an occasional small swamp, and lots of red clay. The corn is thin and unhealthy; an occasional oil well, some rail fences, lots of wild flowers, and small Negro shacks all along the way ... Glenn

Diary 6-25-1918

Nothing to do except try to keep cool and perspire, a natural result of the Texas heat. Haven't seen a horn toad or lizard for two days.

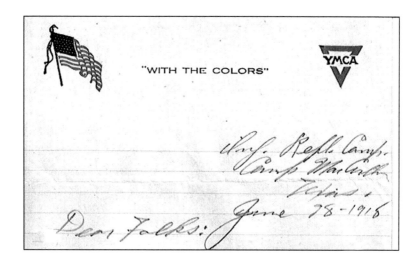

Letter 6-28-1918

Infantry Replacement Camp, MacArthur, Texas
Dear Folks,

I also received orders today to report to Camp Bowie, Texas (Fort Worth) for duty with the 142nd Infantry, so kindly change my address to that place.
Glenn

Diary 7-1-1918

Reported to the 36th Division 142 Infantry and was assigned to 71st Brigade Co. A for duty. Spent most of the day looking over the grounds as well as the political atmosphere of Oklahoma and Texas National Guard.

During the previous fall (1917), the 36th Division was organized following the War Department's newly published "Table of Organization." The new 36th Division incorporated 18,000 members of the Texas National Guard and 2,500 Guardsmen from Oklahoma. Over the next several months 8,500 draftees were added. As expected, there were immediate intrastate jealousies compounding other "inharmonious elements."

The Division Commander and his staff were Regular Army. They and the subordinate Guardsmen had not yet developed the mutual respect that would later evolve. Further tension was introduced by the arrival of a large number of freshly trained Reserve officers (among whom was Glenn).

The National Guard officers had hometown loyalties and biases, but they had also worked hard and frequently spent considerable money from their own pockets in organizing and equipping their units. They rather resented the presence of these new officers. The Reserve officers had a different background. They had completed a very strenuous training to secure their commissions. They had little respect for the National Guard officers who, they perceived, obtained their commissions largely through political influence.

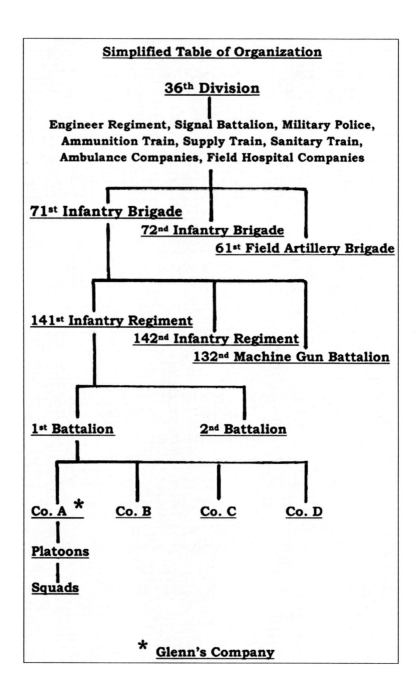

Simplified Table of Organization

36th Division

Engineer Regiment, Signal Battalion, Military Police,
Ammunition Train, Supply Train, Sanitary Train,
Ambulance Companies, Field Hospital Companies

71st Infantry Brigade

72nd Infantry Brigade

61st Field Artillery Brigade

141st Infantry Regiment

142nd Infantry Regiment

132nd Machine Gun Battalion

1st Battalion

2nd Battalion

Co. A *

Co. B

Co. C

Co. D

Platoons

Squads

* **Glenn's Company**

The reorganization went forward slowly but steadily and was "completed," on paper at least, by October 15, 1917. In the months of hard training that followed, old prejudices gradually diminished.

Organizing and training the new division was extremely difficult. Some of the men arrived still in civilian clothes and many had little or no previous training. Initially, the men drilled and did guard duty with sticks and clubs. It was weeks before they were all in uniform and even longer before they were issued their rifles and other equipment.

When Glenn arrived at Camp Bowie his days were devoted to organizing the company, incorporating the newly assigned soldiers, and getting their equipment in order. In a short time he became familiar with the chain of command. Glenn also discovered that many of the officers had indeed been appointed on the basis of local politics and many of them were not at all keen about active duty.

Texas National Guard Shoulder Patch.

Glenn E. Miller Collection
Camp Bowie, Texas.

Inoculation Card.

16. On the Way

Diary 7-10-1918

> Loaded all the company property in the morning and made the final police of the Camp Inspection. Inspected the rifles and left Camp Bowie via T & P [Texas & Pacific Railroad] at 5:20 going east.

Diary 7-11 thru 16-1918

> Shreveport. Crossed the Miss. River at Vicksburg at 7 pm, then Albany, Birmingham and Blue Ridge with shacks, saw mills and smelters. (Passed through) Atlanta in the night time, into South Carolina by morning. Raleigh, the canteen women are good entertainers and spirit of the south is hard to beat, Sunday awoke at Richmond, then to Washington, Baltimore, Wilmington, Philadelphia, Trenton, arrived in N. Y. 11 pm. Awoke the next morning in Long Island Railroad yards ... and spent most of the day getting to camp and unloading. Here it is rumored that the 1st Battalion's ship is laid up for repairs so we will be a day or so late in leaving.

Glenn E. Miller Collection

**Glenn's Full Pack,
Ready for Inspection.**

Letter   7-26-1918

142nd Infantry, Camp Mills, New York

Dear Folks,

My "Indiana" girl asked me for mother's address in one of her letters, but I forgot to send it to her. So in case you do hear from her, treat her courteous but don't give her any encouragement for she certainly doesn't need any as she has assumed more now than is good for her. ... We are now wearing our overseas caps and have the appearance of a bunch of Canadians.

Your loving son, Glenn

Diary 7-30-1918

Camp Milles N.Y.

Up early and over to station. Trains to New York, ferry to Hoboken and loaded at noon on U. S. S. Maui. Assigned to stateroom #117.

Glenn's Official Identification Card.

All the troops aboard addressed postcards to their families having them ready to mail as soon as they landed in France. The card was preprinted, "Ship on which I sailed has arrived safely overseas."

In the previous fall, the first of a stream of troopships bulging with soldiers left Hoboken for Brest, France, a seven or eight day crossing. The ships were organized into convoys so they could be better protected from submarine attacks. "Glenn's" convoy was protected by a cruiser and two destroyers. But not all the crossings went well.

There were frequent torpedo attacks. The *George Washington*, the *President Lincoln*, and the *Leviathan* and the *Maui* were among those ships that successfully crossed the Atlantic. Not so for the *Baltic, Tuscania, Moldovia,* and *Ticonderoga,* each of which was sent to the bottom by German torpedoes.

Diary 8-1-1918

Still sea-sick and relieved from guard. My bunk is my best friend and hoping that I have the inherited qualities of a seaman as Grandfather Kean was a sailor.

Diary 8-3-1918

Maneuvering all morning and about noon had a little gun practice and judging from the splash we are safe. That is if we get the first shot

Diary 8-4-1918

Sunday.
The most beautiful Sunday I have ever spent on the Ocean. Spent most of the day reading magazines. A convoy of 22 ships appears on our Port side.

Diary 8-8-1918

> Sea gulls are seen with the first rays of the morning sun . . . a strong wind and plenty of heavy seas, which developed into a squall. Eight days out and say, why try to kid one another; a dust storm would look good.

Diary 8-10-1918

> Our fleet protection joined us this morning, ten small destroyers, and what a sense of safety they brought with them.

Diary 8-11-1918

> Sunday.
> A submarine scare, two some say, and after a few shots it performed a nose dive to the bottom of the sea. Now official. Hit a nest of sub-marines in the afternoon and a torpedo only missed us by a few yards out of all the shots and maneuvers.

Diary 8-12-1918

> Saw land about breakfast time and docked during the morning at the Port of Brest, France. Unloaded during the afternoon and marched to Pontanezen Barracks.

17. Across France

In mid-1918 a dust storm at the Cavalry's Fort Riley in Kansas whipped up huge clouds of dust originating from widespread piles of horse manure. The dust sent hundreds of coughing, stumbling soldiers to the post hospital. The diagnosis was highly infectious influenza, although some claimed it was a resurgence of the plague. A pandemic raced through the Army and spread to nearby civilians. As one of the troopships arrived at Brest it was reported that 200 men had died and were buried at sea and 4,000 of the troops were disabled by the sickness. The contagion spread into Europe, striking civilians, and French, British, and German soldiers as well.

In September, 142,000 American men scheduled for induction were given a reprieve because of the pandemic. In Europe, General Pershing made an urgent but unsuccessful plea for more men because within his A.E.F. 150,000 were stricken. Toward the end of October the influenza faded, but the fatality rate was appalling. Influenza was eventually identified as the cause of death for one-third of all Americans who died in the war.

After unloading from the U.S.S. *Maui*, Lt. Miller's division spent the next several days organizing their equipment and preparing to move east toward the staging area to the rear of the battle lines.

Diary 8-19-1918

Loaded on the train at Brest and started east, forty men to a box car – not even room for both feet on the floor at the same time. The route looks like a straight line to Versailles, near Paris.

Diary 8-20-1918

Still going east, eating corn willie [62] and whatever else we can get. Oh yes, we slept last night, a bit late at night a soldier was killed, riding on top of a box car, he struck a tunnel.

Diary 8-21-1918

Unloaded about 4 am at Bar-Sur-Aube had a light breakfast and then hiked 14 miles to Urville arrived about 3 pm. In the evening Division Inspector was here finding out why so much straggling. He told me how the war broke out as well as several other things.

---

[62] Army slang for corned beef hash.

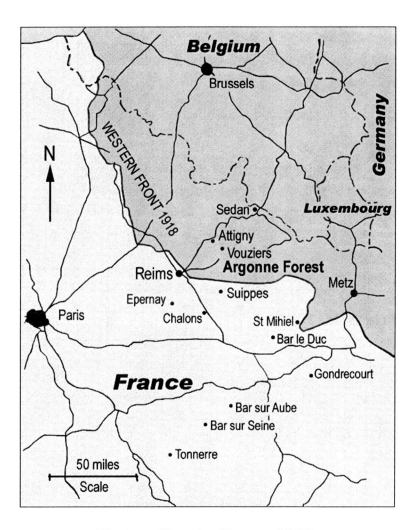

Western Front – France 1918.

Diary 8-22-1918

Major General Smith paid us a visit in the morning and with it lots of hell, so had to spend the day getting cleaned up and located. Started drilling at 2 pm. Took Company over to Bligney for a bath in the evening.

Diary 8-23-1918

Took a detail of fifty men into Bar-Sur-Aube to be transferred to 42nd Div. Had my hands full in keeping them together and trying to feed them. Slept an hour or so but spent the night on a side hill in the rain. New battalion Commander reports, the same man as of August 21, 1918.

Diary 8-24-1918

Got relieved from the responsibility of my detail at 8 am, so cleaned up and got back to Urville tired and hungry but still on my feet.

American Expeditionary Force

Dear Folks,

I presume that you wonder where I am and what I am doing so will tell you all I can – first we have moved – we stayed about a week at the last Camp, Pontanezen, near Brest, then moved by rail. ... It was quite a trip on these French Railroads side door cars – with the men forty to a box car and only twenty ton cars at that. Well it did get pretty tiresome at that.

We are now where the grapes grow on side hills and in stony ground. Talk about not raising anything in land, well here they grow grapes in rocks. In fact they are so thick with rock that a rainstorm doesn't wash any dirt on a side hill, but that is quite off the subject.

We are at our training now and it is like the days at Fort Snelling. All I have to do is to work like hell from 5:30 am until 9 pm and then study a couple of hours after that. But they haven't even dented me yet for I have increased about an inch and a half around the waist and getting harder than a ... "Well name it yourself." But anyway I am still going good and feel fine.

For the first few days we landed here I was the only officer on duty with the company and I sure did buzz around. We are billeted in a small inland town about 9 miles from the railroad so you see the white lights don't bother us any, in fact we can't even get oil to burn so we use candles. But that didn't bother any of us.

---

[63] APO, Army Post Office.

Oh yes, it is very pleasant sleeping here as it gets quite cool in the evening and rather warm in the middle of the day. In fact yesterday morning my feet got cold while marching to the rifle range. Yet in the afternoon my nose got blistered from the sun. So you see we wear the overseas cap like the Canadians and so have no protection for the face or eyes.

Have my winter clothes all lined up for action. Oh yes, you remember that raincoat I had when on leave, well, I cut out a perfectly good blanket the other evening and made a wool interliner for it and so have a dandy trench coat as they call them. After I fit it, I had a French woman sew a few buttons in place and so I can detach it according to the weather. ... Sunday is a name almost lost to my vocabulary, but I have hope of soon regaining it.

Your loving son Glenn

New Hazards

Letter 9-5-1918 APO

My Dear Miss Goehry,

We are now billeted in a small French town about 12 miles from the railroad and quite a way behind the line, though occasionally we can hear a big gun. ... Takes every minute from 5 am to 9 pm and sometimes longer, never shorter. We are however allowed an hour Sunday morning to take a bath in a nearby lake at which time we hold foot inspection and a lecture about sanitation. Was paid today, all in French money – have enough to paper a room in sizes from a few inches square to one the size of a big poster.

Sincerely yours,   Glenn.

Sanitation was a major concern. The mud in the trenches and across the battlefields was not just dirt. It was saturated with anaerobic bacteria. The European mud was laced with decomposing human waste and animal remains. Bacterial contamination was widespread and led to septic poisoning. A tiny wound was enough to endanger a soldier's life.

Along with the septic poisoning was the infestation of rats. But at least the soldiers could see them. Along with the threat to soldiers' health they provided a diversionary challenge to the trench occupants. All sorts of tricks were used to lure them out of their hiding places so they could be bayoneted.

Letter 9-8-1918 APO

My Dear Martha,   [Goehry]

This is quite a place here and affords quite a bit of curiosity as one of the boys said. They have mostly two wheeled wagons the reason being they want to make another wagon with the other two wheels. They also hitch their horses one ahead of the other and drive them mostly by talking to them. Oh yes, the town crier just went down the street beating a drum – when he gets to the corner he gives out the latest war dope. And so goes their funny ways.

Sincerely Glenn

Letter 9-19-1918 APO

Dear Martha,   [Goehry]

The rainy season or winter seems to be starting and so adds a bit more to our inconvenience. For the boys have only one suit at present. Our steel helmets do however protect us from the shock and also keep our heads dry. We have a model that keeps their shape well and the style hasn't changed since our first issue. Gas masks have become a part of our lives, for we cannot appear without them – to do so is an unpardonable sin and means extra hours.   Sincerely, Glenn

This rather casual reference to gas masks is undoubtedly to avoid revealing the soldiers' high anxiety about it and to minimize the worries for the folks at home. Earlier in the war when the Western Front was locked in a stalemate, both sides were looking for a breakout strategy. In 1915 the Germans unleashed gas warfare. Along the Canadian sector soldiers watched as a thick, low hanging mist of yellow-green chlorine began drifting toward their lines and settling in their trenches. Thousands of men scrambled out of their trenches and ran for the rear, clutching at their throats leaving an 8,000 yard undefended gap in the line. The gas attack was horribly successful, with the hundreds of gas's first victims lying dead with clenched fists.

In the initial gas attacks, the gas used was a form of chlorine. It causes the body to overproduce secretions in the lungs so that the victim drowns in his own fluids. Since the chlorine is soluble in water the British devised a crude but effective solution, water-soaked rags tied around the nose and mouth. Urine was used if needed.

By the end of 1915 the Germans switched to phosgene, which is many times more powerful than chlorine and causes death through suffocation. The Allies' defensive response was a grotesque gas mask with huge goggles and a canister with a filter dangling below. One German technique was to first explode bombs containing fine powder, which clogged the gas mask filters making them unusable. When soldiers threw away their unusable masks the Germans exploded the phosgene bombs.

Gas Mask with Filter Canister.

18. Into the Trenches

Late In September 1918 the Allies marshaled 260,000 men with which to launch the major Meuse-Argonne offensive. The attack was unleashed early morning on Sept 26th. Along a twenty-five mile long front 3,980 artillery pieces broke the air with flashes of blinding light and deafening roar. The artillery was designed to clear out the German trenches and open the way for the attacking Allied troops.

Letter 9-30-1918 APO 796

Dear Folks,

The country here is not quite as rough as it was at our last station. Our move however was not very far, though at the present we can hear the big guns and see the flash. The other afternoon witnessed an air battle at great distance. Am getting plenty to eat and a place to sleep. Have been resting a few days, no bugle calls and sleeping until eight is quite a treat. Guess my "Indiana" girl has started correspondence with sister Enid. I received quite a few letters from her.

Sincerely Glenn

Under French Command

To back up the front line Glenn's 36th Division moved to the area between Epernay and Chalons. They trained here for 10 days awaiting their battle orders.

Glenn E. Miller Collection
Trenches at the Rear.

In coordinating commands with the other Allied nations, the French and British wanted to assign individual American troops to serve as replacements in the French or British Armies. General Pershing strongly resisted, citing the difficulty with language differences, insisted that the Americans serve in their own organized units. He felt even more strongly that in doing so the American effort would be better recognized and appreciated.

However, General Pershing did agree that organized units of U.S. Army could operate under French Army command. As a result, on October 3, 1918, in preparation for the Meuse-Argonne offensive, the entire 36th Division was transferred to the Fourth French Army.

A few days later, as the 36th Division was on the march toward the front lines, the commander of Company A "dropped out because of fatigue" and Glenn was ordered to take command of the company.

Glenn E. Miller Collection
Trenches with Dugout.

The Allied offensive was well underway as the American troops approached their assigned sector of the Argonne Forest. The French, on their right, had not yet taken Medeah Farm. It was a perfect haven for machine-guns bearing on the Regulars' flank. The Germans, in this section, were fighting hard to make up for the easy surrender of their comrades on Blanc-Monte.

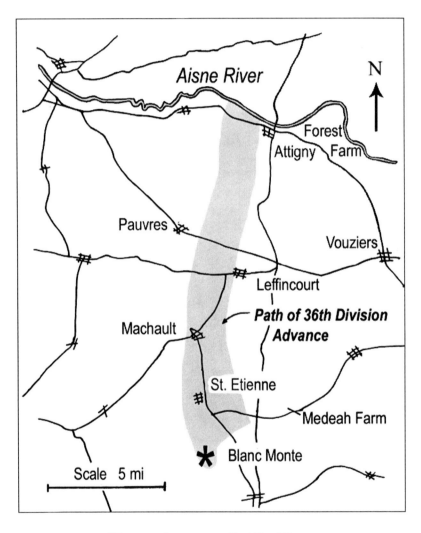

**Meuse-Argonne Battle Map.
Path of 36th Infantry Advance
from Blanc Monte to Aisne River.**

The next landmarks in the path of the Regulars' progress were the ridges in front of the village of St. Etienne. Here the defenders refused to be stampeded. The German artillery fire was furious throughout October 5. Early on the morning of October 6, under a hurricane barrage, a regiment of Regulars and one of the Marines, side-by-side, set out to take the last ridge before St. Etienne. This meant that somehow the defenses had to be broken. It was one of the occasions when the troops charged, ignoring the tremendous odds against them. They took the ridge with a loss estimated at 30 per cent and dug in.

It had been a grueling fifth day of non-stop battle for the Regulars, who seemed be at the limit of their endurance. Relief for them was due. On the night of October 6 the 36th Division began arriving. Comprised of the National Guard from Texas and Oklahoma, they had never been under fire before. Its fresh and inexperienced battalions were now mixed with the tired battalions of the 2nd to learn warfare first-hand from the Regulars and Marines, and from the battle-hardened Germans who were in a very ugly mood.

After a day of reorganizing and digging, a regiment of the 36th charged St. Etienne on the morning of October 8. The French were reported to have patrols in the town, but it was very much still in the hands of the enemy machine gunners. They had positioned themselves in the adjoining cemetery, which gave them a free sweep of fire across an open field without any cover whatsoever.For half a kilometer the men of the 36th kept their line even with the veterans. The Marines entered the town while the men of the 36th were still in the open.

Glenn E. Miller Collection
Open Ground Across St. Etienne Cemetery.

It was the 36th Division's first taste of machine-gun nests. They had no experience to judge the extraordinary intensity of fire. Their orders were to keep on going, and they did so. In front of them, as they crossed the open field, was a wooded ravine. Their artillery had no appreciable effect on the German machine gunners which were sending a tornado of bullets into the Division's advance, in addition to a shower of shells from the German guns.

The Southwesterners who were meeting both bullets and shells for the first time did not fall back before the deadly combination of artillery and machine-gun fire. In their fierce charge, the 36th lost a third of their numbers.

Glenn E. Miller Collection.
The Results of Artillery Fire.

Meanwhile, the French had taken Medeah Farm but were still well back of St. Etienne. All day of October 9 was spent re-forming the 36th's position but the Germans, showing no signs of withdrawal, counter-attacked the French beyond Medeah Farm.

The American 36th Division who now took up the battle were assigned the tired artillery of the 2nd as they had no guns of their own. They lacked horses, transport, and nearly everything a Division should have except rifles in the hands of men who knew how to use them. On the morning of October 10 their reconnaissance showed that the enemy artillery and machine-gun fire was as powerful as ever.

It was hardly a situation in which an inexperienced Division should begin a movement in the dark, but with the French being ready to advance on the left, the 36th began an attack that evening.

The Germans, already preparing for retreat, still had large forces of field artillery in range. Evidently, they were determined to take revenge on these new troops by a prolonged bombardment, expending as much of their ammunition as they could instead of leaving it behind to be captured. The accurate and moving sheet of shell fire which the Germans laid down on the advancing infantry of the 36th was designed to instill pure panic. There was bound to be some disorganization, but there was no faltering. Pressing on as they closed up gaps, the charging units took the Machault.

The enemy resistance had suddenly broken. After this final spasm of reprisal, all German guns were moving fast to the Aisne, bridges were destroyed, and machine-gun nests established north of the river. The Germans were obviously preparing to make another stand.

The advancing 36th Division did not waste time with the machine-gunners who attempted rear-guard action. Instead, they raced ahead for fifteen miles in a single day. When they reached the south side of the Aisne River they busied themselves in swimming across on scouting trips and actively sniping at individual enemy troops across the river.

At a bend in the river the Germans still held a heavily fortified defensive position at Forest Farm. It was protected by machine-gun emplacements, barbed wire entanglements, and was overlooked by artillery from the hills north of the river

Allied attacks on Forest Farm the night of October 16 and 17 had both failed. The next attack had to be different. It started on October 27 with a concentration of artillery firing high explosives to neutralize the Germans artillery, then smoke shells to shield the attacking troops from observation. Three minutes before "H-hour," a creeping artillery barrage raked the open land in front of the troops and blasted through the barbed wire. A machine-gun barrage fired at the same time sent a thick hail of bullets to keep the defenders in their dugouts until the attacking troops were upon them.

After a near perfect offensive maneuver by the 36th the Germans fell back rapidly. The Division was relieved by French troops who pressed ahead and the 36th Division was held in reserve. They had taken 813 prisoners and a German supply depot worth tens of millions of dollars. It had supplied that section of the German line for four years.

The Meuse-Argonne offensive was the 36th Division's only battle, but they had fought it in an exemplary way.

Glenn E. Miller Collection
Church at St. Etienne Used by Germans.

19. Glenn's View

After a few days, Glenn described his experience in the Battle of St. Etienne in letters to both his parents and teacher friend, Martha. His letters remained upbeat and did not reflect the intensity of his battle experiences.

Letter 10-21-1919   **APO**

Dear Folks,

   you may be wondering why you have not heard from me for several weeks and as to where I am located. Well to begin with I am now sitting in a hole in the ground about 4x6-ft. square and 3 ½ feet deep on the back side of a hill. Yes, we have it covered over and camouflaged. Why select such a place for an abode you ask. That it easily answered. It is the best we could find and the safest place in this position.

   As to its selection, let me go back for a period of several weeks and review as briefly as I can the events of the past. When I last wrote I was occupying a room, or rather six of us occupied one room which a German officer occupied four years ago. We were there only a few days when we took trucks toward the front.

COLT AUTOMATIC PISTOL, GOVERNMENT MODEL

SECTIONAL VIEW

METHOD OF OPERATION.   SAFETY DEVICES.

Side Arms Were Carried by All Officers.

After spending a few days in the dugouts of an old French position, we left there on Sunday morning by foot and after marching all day arrived in front of the old Hindenburg line[64], where we left our blankets, had a meal of bully beef and hard bread, and again took up the march.

Our guide lost his way[65] and for this reason it took us all night to get into position. It being a rather chilly night and our first experience under big shell fire, you can imagine about how we felt. We reached our

---

[64] The Hindenburg Line was a vast system of German defenses across northeastern France. The fortifications included concrete bunkers and machine gun emplacements, heavy lines of barbed wire, deep trenches, and dugouts. In front of the fortifications were broad open fields for exposing any attackers.

[65] The French guide was familiar with the terrain; however, the foot soldiers were led along circuitous pathways through the forest. The narrow roads, with their profusion of mud holes, were reserved for the movement of artillery and ammunition.

positions about daybreak, and each man dug himself a hole for safety, and there we spent the day.

We were a kilometer and a half behind the front lines. At four o'clock Tuesday morning [October 8] we received orders to be ready to move out on a minute's notice. At 5:15 am we were ordered to go over the top, which we did. We hit the front line and before long the whole regiment was involved in taking a big nest of machine guns. It was a day spent amidst lead and iron, and one I shall never forget.

We took quite a large number of prisoners and captured their positions. "Fritz" fell back lightly but still sent over an abundance of "keep-your-head-downs." We held this position for the next two days and Thursday night we were favored with a gas attack and plenty of shells. Friday morning a fresh regiment "leap-frogged" us but during the night "Fritz" had withdrawn, so we had to follow him up for twenty kilometers, our regiment now being in support. We stayed in position Friday however, and Saturday advanced in the rain and mud, spending the night under a few twigs and resting most of Sunday. [66]

Wishing to spend the day as is the custom among some people in the states, that is to clean up a bit, I secured an extra canteen of water, about a quart. With this I washed my hands, face, and ears and with the water left I took a shave, and so felt refreshed, after the first wash-up I had had in a week. Not wishing to

---

[66] Glenn was awarded the French Croix de Guerre for his valor during this offensive.

neglect the other extreme of my body I took off my shoes, a process I had almost forgotten, and exposed my feet to the sun, as this was the best bath available. After a bath it is usually a good plan to change clothes, so I took the sock off my right foot and put it on my left. Oh yes I forgot to mention we got a hot meal, the first in a week's time.

Sunday afternoon we moved forward and our regiment took up a front line position, my battalion being in regimental reserve. We spent the rest of Sunday, Monday and Tuesday here. No shells were falling now, but a nice drizzling rain. On Wednesday evening we moved, ... up to a front line position, where we have remained ever since.

Saturday I took a patrol forward to gain contact with the enemy, which was easily accomplished and for most of the night we moved along the canal, the Aisne River, crossing our entire front, finding out what we had ahead of us. Sunday evening our company exchanged positions with one of the others and so we now have a position a little better protected. I improved the opportunity to get a little sleep here taking my shoes off and what a treat.

Today I secured a pair of clean socks and feel like I have had my Christmas. Oh yes, last Thursday we received our mail. I got nineteen letters and a copy of the Ravenna News. Tell Pa Cass[67] that the News has quite a circulation, for I left it within throwing distance of the enemy and twenty five miles from Belgian soil. For covers at night I use my heavy coat. We are now getting

---

[67] The Ravenna News Editor.

two hot meals a day, and so enjoy the outings. We are all in splendid health although exposed to the weather. We are all expecting victory and are feeling fine.

Yes, by the way, most of the boys have 'em - at least I am certain of one who has. ["cooties"] You know what I mean – those things that crawl and keep you awake at nights, [lice, cooties] but wait till I catch the leader and if I don't paint him up so the rest will chase themselves to death, it will be because I can't get any red, white and blue paint. Tomorrow we move back in reserve and four days rest.

Your son, Lieut. Glenn E. Miller,

"Dog Tag" for

Glenn E Miller 1st Lt.
142 Inf O.R.C.

Glenn E. Miller Collection

Adding to the Misery.

The Doughboys called them "cooties" (body lice). They clung to clothing with tiny claws while sucking blood from their host. Their itch was pervasive. If a man scratched himself he soon had bleeding sores that became infected. Soldiers stripped to search the seams of their clothing to find them but it was losing battle, as each louse laid several nearly invisible eggs a day. The best relief, the delousing van, invariably arrived on the coldest day. Soldiers stripped down and threw their clothing into a steam tank where the lice and their eggs were boiled to death while the soldiers vigorously scrubbed down. Still, relief was short-lived.

In 1918 the Germans had advanced their gas weaponry with a fearsome and stubborn new agent: mustard gas. The gas is heavier than air and settles into craters and trenches. However, since the spread of any gas relies on the wind, its use was a risky thing. On several occasions a shift of wind returned the gas right back over to the attackers. The mustard gas terrorized the soldiers and the gas masks alone were insufficient protection. The gas burns and blisters any exposed part of the body and has long-term effects. It swells the eyelids causing blindness, causes deafness, and inability to swallow, choking, and difficulty breathing. And there is no known treatment for mustard gas exposure.

Letter 10-26-1918   APO 796

Dear Folks,

We moved back as I expected and have been in reserve for several days - expect to move forward and in support for several days and then to the front line again, a sort of rotation, but then again we hope to be relieved in a day or so – then to a rest camp and reorganize again ... and again on the go.

Your loving son, Glenn

1st Lt. Glenn E. Miller.

20. Armistice Signed

When Glenn's Division was relieved at Attigny on the Aisne River, they were transferred from the French 4th Army back to the U.S. First, and moved to the Conde-en-Barie area – 20 miles southwest of Reims. There the Army was preparing for another offensive.

At the same time, negotiations for an Armistice were being held in a railroad car parked on a siding forty miles from Paris. Communications were difficult, with messages and replies slow in reaching the negotiators. Many parties were pressing for a cease-fire while the negotiations were underway but the Generals, most notably Pershing, did not want to stop. He maintained, "There can be no conclusion to this war until Germany has been brought to her knees." He wanted to compel an unconditional surrender.

The Armistice agreement finally hammered out required an extensive list of humiliating German concessions both military and political. Mindful of the continuing slaughter of troops on both sides there was a plea from many officers for a cease-fire immediately after signing.

But the Armistice agreement called for the cease-fire at 11 A.M. on November 11, 1918. Despite the announcement early in the morning, previously issued orders to attack stood unchanged. The firing continued unabated. Allied artillery crews expressed a gritty reality in those last hours as they pumped out shells as fast as they could. They did not want to be saddled with many rounds of dangerous live ammunition to deal with afterwards.

Twenty six thousand, 26,000, men of the A.E.F. were killed in the Meuse-Argonne offensive – the greatest loss of life in a single battle up to that date. And the killing continued in those brief hours after the Armistice was signed. Before it went into effect, 320 more soldiers lost their lives.

Glenn E. Miller Collection

Damage from Artillery Shelling.

Letter 11-19-1918   APO

My Dear Martha,

   You may be rather surprised that you have not heard from me for such a period of time, but such have been the course of events that the occasion was not always right for letter writing.

   Well, to review briefly the past, we went into the line Oct the 6th – that is we marched all day and night of the sixth on one cold meal and into position early the morning of the seventh and went over on the morning of the eighth. Well for three days, words fail me when I go to describe them. The first day we attacked and the next two we straightened the line and held – then a twenty two kilometer advance and again into position, and ready to push forward again but we were too far ahead of our flanks and couldn't. The weather was chilly and very damp – we slept in holes dug in the ground, for protection from the big shells and shrapnel, about three feet deep and long enough to stretch out in. For covering we had the blue sky and it was usually cloudy and falling mist or rain. The first week we lived on salvage – that is what we could pick up from packs of the dead men and those left by the wounded. In all, we spent twenty one days in close contact before we were relieved.

   One night I led a patrol along the River Aisne at Attigny thru the village and along the river and never will I forget that night for snipers were shooting at us from across the river and so desperate were they to stop the Americans that field artillery pieces were used. After our withdrawal we spent several days in reserve resting and although we had only the bare building of a deserted French village, yet rest we did as three weeks is a long time to spend without even taking off your shoes. From there we took a six day hike to another French town where we have just finished two weeks of intensive training during which time the event of all events happened [the Armistice] and such a feeling of gladness as is in the heart of every American soldier.

While at our period of training we had only two officers on duty and with about eighty men to break in you can imagine how busy I have been. So, kindly excuse my long delay.

Two days ago I was ordered to attend the First Corp School and great is my joy for such has been my wish ever since I landed in France. And just as I was leaving orders came for the division to move and so when school is through, in four weeks, I will find them in a different location. Their orders were for a five day march but I couldn't find out to what point. Some rumors that we were one of the Occupation Divisions other, that we were headed for a southern port but neither suits me as they may starve us and fail to clothe us, yet the bullets won't be whizzing and so we will enjoy it.

Now I did not intend to take up so much space telling of myself. My intentions were to plead for pardon for the long delay, so kindly be gracious. What we will do now I cannot say.

I sincerely hope you are enjoying Washington and will have a political pull by the time I get out of the Army for I'll be in need of a job unless I take up an old "calling" and that is too quiet after the past few months.

I can earnestly say that several letters you wrote to me and that I received on the front line brought me more real joy than a hot meal and that's going some. Let the good work go on. I will write you more in a day or so. I will be at the same old address.

Sincerely Glenn

Letter November 24, 1918

Dear Dad,

As this seems to be the day set aside for Dad Day, here goes. One thing nice about it is that the censorship ban has been lifted and so I can tell you of some of my past experiences. ...When we went into the line we marched from Suippes, which is up near Chalons, to Somme. There we left our packs and went about a mile south of a small town by the name of St. Etienne. Here we did our fighting for three days, thence forward to Attigny we were south of the river and they on the North bank – here it was a question of trying to force our patrols across the river with Germans sniffing at us. I had one of these patrols but I gained contact with the enemy without crossing the canal or river and so didn't have to swim – when we were relieved up here we marched to Hargerville which is another small town about six miles north of Bar-le-Duc.

While stationed here I was sent up to Gondrecourt to the First Corps School, about thirty miles southeast of Bar-le-Duc. Our division has since moved farther south and will be someplace near Bar-sur-Seine.

Going farther back I left Hoboken on the 31st of July – landed at Brest August 12th, sailing on the U. S. S. Maui – stayed a week at the Pontanezen Barracks, where Napoleon received his military education, we then moved straight east to Bur-sur-Aube where we spent our training period until about the middle of September then moved to a little town about half way between Chalons and Epernay. Stayed here about ten days and thence to Suippes by truck and the rest as previously mentioned.

In our fight our regiment only had a hundred and seventy six killed and about forty five hundred wounded, but I never received a scratch – had just as much to eat [i.e. incoming gun fire] as the rest of them and was farther forward than the most of them. We were then with the 4th French Army and when we came out of the line were transferred to the 1st American. We were ready to travel on the 10th of November but were held up and with the signing of the Armistice our orders were cancelled. We were headed for the Argonne forest which would have meant stiff fighting.

Oh yes, School here being delayed a week. We were all given a pass to Paris and so spent two days there last week. It's some city but as such can't compare with American cities. Its subways are good but not very extensive. Street cars are not as numerous as might be but their taxis cabs are numerous and the cheapest thing a man can spend his money for. The buildings are mostly under eight stories and although they have several large department stores, the chief one around is "Louvre" which I went there. Yet most of them are small shops. Haven't yet collected any souvenirs but will try to get a few small ones before we ship back to the States, which of course I don't know when but don't believe will be before spring. Wishing you all the best of Holiday Greetings, I beg to remain

      Your loving son, Glenn

Glenn E. Miller Collection
A "Rest and Recreation" Ride.

Glenn E. Miller Collection

Glenn Has His Portrait Taken in Paris.

21. After the Armistice

Letter 12-9-1918   APO

My dear Martha,

Received a letter from you yesterday forwarded from the Company and can honestly say that it was more than appreciated. You seem to be enjoying yourself as well as seeing the sights. Your poems on the flu and the war worker are just splendid and were enjoyed by all the boys who read them. Have been having a good time, yet we don't do very much except a little maneuver in the morning and a couple of lectures in the afternoon. Have a band concert or a movie three or four times a week so manage to spend most of our evenings that way.

The States may be dry but we are still able to get a little champagne, wine and beer over here though the price is high and the flavor foreign but far be it from me to indulge – of course somebody has to sample it before it can be distributed.

What is that young sister of yours doing? You know you haven't mentioned her name for a long time. Also give my regards to Helen W. Am looking forward to another trip to Paris as one only gets to know where to go on the first trip.

Yours, Glenn

Letter 12-26-1918

Carisey, France.

My Dear Martha,

We left school on Monday and I reported back Tuesday. Well to my sorrow I found out that during my absence that I had been transferred to company E, so here I am among strangers. I did manage to get back to my old company for Christmas. Had a big dinner at noon, then came back here and here the officers put on a real spread – orchestra, meal served in courses, a different drink with every course. Then we repaired to a clearing in a barn where the queens of the village had been corralled. Thus with company and music, the dance started but after watching the maddened throng for several numbers, I decided that I wasn't quite, no you can't call it that, you know it wasn't quite the right kind of liquor to make me dance with the "frogs," so I excused myself and retired at nine, a very late hour for me. Others stayed way into the night. You see, I prefer to associate with prize waltzers – you know who I mean.

Sincerely yours, Glenn

A French Croix de Guerre

Glenn E. Miller Collection

Chateau de Vaux, Carisey.

Letter 1-9-1919

My dear Martha,   Carisey, France.

As I told you before here I am in my new company, E with the Indians; John Mankiller, Pete Maytubby, Alexander Chuculate and Rising Bear, with lots more – but they are all fine soldiers and willing workers.[68]

Am not very busy now, all I have to do besides my regular company duty is to be supply officer, handle all the bad hombres of the company, have charge of the Regimental Rifle Range and be Battalion School

---

[68] In later years Glenn told his family about the Choctaw soldiers. With telephone wires strung out every which way across the battlefield, the lines were frequently tapped by opposing forces. The Choctaw were used as "code talkers," speaking in their native dialect to relay messages and orders. Their lexicon included many uniquely Choctaw terms: cannon fire was "big thunder," a casualty was "scalp," a machine gun was "little gun shoot fast," the 3rd battalion was "three grains of corn."

Officer. You see even though I leave home and travel to the other side of the globe, I didn't get away from the old occupation at which we both used to work. Have two schools, one of about forty and the other one of seventy five.

Had a big time New Years. Lifted the ban and so true to the French custom, you have to take a drink with everybody when you wish them a Happy New Year. Another custom they have is, when you wished them a Happy New Year is to kiss them on both cheeks, but this I balked at. Although they are nice girls in this town they spend their time herding cattle or sheep and wear wooden shoes. – Sufficient description is to say that it was a true pattern after our own real country dance.

My present abode is about 15 kilometers west of Tonnerre, in Yonne. Yes this is, no what? No sunny France for the sun only shows its face once a week and the other days it rains. If you notice that the boys of the A. E. F. have a peculiar walk, you will know that they have web feet.

Sincerely, Glenn

A French Croix de Guerre

Carisey, France.

My dear Martha,

Just returned from trip to Nice which you know is famous as a Southern resort. My leave was for 10 days and while there I made several sightseeing trips along the sea and into the country. Going down we traveled first class on an American special train I visited east along the sea, taking the rubber-neck wagon or auto until we arrived at the famous province of Monaco. Here is located the world famous Monte Carlo where money changes hands very fast.

To the left is the yard of the prince's palace which is quite a lovely spot. We also visited the aquarium, stopping for dinner or lunch at the Hotel Venice, thence onward toward Italy (which you see in the background). The change is very gradually and one does not note the change of nationality. Notice how the hillsides are cultivated. I then had my picture taken with my back toward France. Thence home by the hills of this ruin of an ancient Roman castle.

Thence to Nice, and although the scenery is very beautiful and the sights are many, my brief review is but a glimpse for it is the most wonderful I have ever taken. ...From there we go up into the canyon – visit a small village of but 47 persons and God only knows how many goats ... onto the city of Grasse, where we visited a perfumery and thence home, tired but happy after a very enjoyable day.

Sincerely yours, Glenn

Glenn E. Miller Collection

**Co. E, 142nd Infantry,
Carisey, Yonne, France.
1st Lt. Glenn Miller, at arrow.**

The French *Croix de Guerre*

On April 3, 1919, at a Dress Parade for General Pershing and French Marshall Petain, various members of the 36th Division were recognized for their service. Glenn was awarded the French *Croix de Guerre* with a Bronze Star for his leadership, "bravery and courage" in the Meuse-Argonne Offensive.

After he returned home he was also awarded the United States Victory Medal with a Bar for service in the Defensive Sector of the A.E.F. and a Bar for his leadership in the Meuse-Argonne Offensive.

French
Croix de Guerre
with Bronze Star.

U.S.
Victory Medal with
Meuse-Argonne Bar
and
Defensive Sector Bar.

CROIX DE GUERRE

Lieutenant Glenn E. Miller, 142nd Infantry.
An officer of great bravery, he enthused his men
during a long advance, encouraging them by his
audacity and courage. They attained all the
objectives assigned to him.
At General Headquarters, the 3rd of April 1919
The Marshall,
Commander in Chief of the French Armies

Petain

22. Coming Home

For the American soldiers World War I lasted about two years – from the time training started in the U. S. until the troops began arriving back home from France.

Letter 4-22-1919

Carisey, France

My dear Martha,

The late rumor is that we are going to start the homeward trip pretty soon. You see it all started like this, first we have a big review for General Pershing, and he tells me that I have a very good company, and then a few days later we receive notice that we are transferred to the S. O. S. [Services of Supply] on the 15th and that we will move to Le Mans about the latter part of this month, and now we have orders to move on the 2nd of May. In order to make our stay in Le Mans short we are doing a lot of the work back here to be ready to embark.

Yours till we meet again, Glenn

Letter 4-24-1919

Carisey, France,

Dear Folks,

Well, our rumor about moving is coming to look like the real thing, for today we received notice that we would leave here on the 2nd of May for Le Mans and then depart from there on the 13th for an embarkation port, and sail on the 28th for the U.S. Well that all sounds very nice and I hope that it is true for now that we are to go home. I want to get it over as soon as possible. ... We are now having lots of inspections, equipment, kitchens, billets and personal. The latter coming every other day, with a campaign against lice or the cooties as some call them. ...

Your loving son, Glenn

Glenn E. Miller Collection

Palace in Monte Carlo.

Letter 5-13-1919

Chateau de Vaux, Yvre' L' E've'que

Dear Folks,

We left Carisey on the 2nd and had a 30 hour run to here. We are now about six kilos east of LeMans and today had our big inspection before leaving for the United States. We are now scheduled to leave here for Brest on the 17th. How long we will stay there I do not know but it should be only a few days. I am not able to tell you at this time whether I will be sent to Camp Bowie with the division or be split up at the Port of Debarkation but will let you know at the first opportunity. If you can secure me several copies of Colliers, April 25th kindly save them for me as it gives a short account of the action of this Division. Will be willing to go to work when I get home, but I don't have any line or business in mind at the present.

Your loving son, Glenn.

Letter 5-13-1919

Chateau de Vaux, Yvre' L'Eve'que,

Dear Martha,

Today we had our big inspection and passed fine I believe. We are now scheduled to leave for Brest on 17th. How long we will be there I do not know, but I hope our stay will be short.

Sincerely yours, Glenn

The entire Division (except for the Artillery) embarked from the port at Brest about May 17. During the Atlantic crossing the ships encountered a severe storm with winds of 96 mph and waves that washed completely across the decks. The troops endured more episodes of sea sickness and two men, from the cruiser *Pueblo*, were washed overboard and drowned, a tragic end for two who had survived the deadly battles with the Germans.

Telegram 5-20-1919

USS Pueblo via NF Newport RI
To: Oscar Miller, Ravenna, Nebraska
New York [on] Saturday morning.
Home [by] middle of June.

Glenn E. Miller Collection

USS *Pueblo*.

Glenn E. Miller Collection

Homeward Bound on Shipboard.

Telegram 5-25-1919

> **Camp Merritt N.J.**
> **To: Oscar Miller, Ravenna, Nebraska.**
> Will leave here tomorrow for Camp Dodge.

They were apparently delayed leaving Camp Merritt.

Telegram 6-2-1919

> Will leave here tomorrow for Camp Dodge.

6-25-1919

> Discharged at Camp Dodge, Iowa.

The Unbelievable Cost

Of Glenn's Company A:
> 156 soldiers actually went into the frontline.
> 8 were killed in action,
> 46 were wounded,
> 24 went on detail to transport ammunition,
>   food, wounded, or to escort prisoners,
> 78 returned from the front.

For the Europeans the war started many months earlier and lasted much longer than it did for the Americans, 1,560 days. The war involved troops and governments of 20 countries. Before an Armistice was reached, 55 million men were mobilized worldwide.

Nearly 9 million soldiers and civilians died and many thousands more were maimed, crippled, or disfigured for life.

With unbelievable good luck Glenn survived, and even escaped injury, despite the horror of 21 days under continuous shelling and rifle fire.

Settling Back As a Civilian

Glenn On Leave at Home in Nebraska.

Well-deserved public gratitude was expressed to those who returned home. Glenn's parents, two brothers, and a sister greeted him warmly. However, other reality of the times soon followed the "Welcome Home" parades. The war had created numerous jobs in the stateside supply-chain producing and transporting equipment and supplies. But as the troops returned home, those jobs ended and jobs for returning Doughboys were elusive.

273

Luckily, Glenn landed a job as a salesman for Nebraska Consolidated Mills. He traveled around Nebraska for almost a year selling flour and feed. This was neither stimulating nor remunerative, but he said, "It was a good way to settle the nerves after Europe."

As he searched for a way to reenter schools and teaching, he jumped at a teaching job to complete a semester at the Greeley, Colorado High School. For the next school year he was hired as High School Principal in his home town, Ravenna. He was now ready for stability. As luck would have it, Nina Hull, a bright and beautiful young woman, was teaching Home Economics there. Predictably, a romance blossomed and they soon married.

Glenn Miller and Nina Hull
Married August 12, 1921.

After three years as Principal, Glenn was elevated to Ravenna School Superintendent, a post he held for ten years. During that time two children were added to their family. In 1929 Glenn earned his Master's degree from the University of Nebraska. He later passed the Bar examination and practiced law for a year.

Glenn's experience as a soldier gave him a deep appreciation of, and kinship with, all returning soldiers. He joined the American Legion, becoming an active and enthusiastic member for many years. In 1935 he was contacted by an American Legion acquaintance from Lexington, Nebraska, inviting him to become Superintendent of Schools there, a position he held until retiring after twenty-one years. Ostensibly retired, he served two years as a Right-of-Way Appraiser for the Interstate highway construction and after that retirement he served a term as Dawson County Judge.

Glenn and other returning soldiers had a kinship and mutual understanding that continued throughout their lifetimes. He never forgot the sacrifices of his fellow soldiers in what was called by many, "The war to end all wars."

The above and the Front Cover pictures are from
America's War for Humanity, **John J. Ingalls, 1898.**

Part IV After Mail Call

Mail call, whether in camp, in a muddy field, or at a lonely outpost, was anxiously awaited. The mail was eagerly read and reread. Often letters were shared with others.

The folks at home seldom understood how tremendously important their letters were to their soldiers in a faraway place.

"I can honestly say that the several letters you wrote me and I received on the front line brought me more real joy than a hot meal."

Glenn Miller, WWI, 1918

Part V Epilogue

While researching conditions under which these three young men resolutely set off to war, I became impressed with their patriotism and willingness to serve their country, as well as with their loyalty and bravery.

At the same time I realized how little they knew or understood the "national interests" that drove their government's actions and how those decisions affected their lives and thousands of others.

With the benefit of hindsight, historians have divulged many private and business interests that influenced those actions, presenting many important "lessons" for those who have followed. However, the "lessons learned" in each war sadly seem to be lost to following generations.

Seemingly, the memory of horrific battlefield deaths and injuries that was so prominent after the **Civil War** dims as generations pass and new wars have replaced it.

The arrogance of the "war lovers"[69] William Randolph Hearst, future president Teddy Roosevelt, and others (congressmen, bankers, businessmen) propelled us into the **Spanish-American War**. Initially, the war was to "protect American interests" in Cuba, but soon it

---

[69] "The War Lovers," Evan Thomas, 2010.

became the United States' "Manifest Destiny" expanding into the Philippines and other Pacific Islands.

Around the turn of the century a web of interlocking alliances triggered **World War I**. Although the United States' entry into the war closely followed the sinking of the liner *Lusitania,* one of the major reasons for the U.S. involvement was to protect millions of dollars loaned by American business to England and other European allies. Then at war's end the crushing peace terms and reparations forced the German civilian population into poverty, creating conditions ripe for the rise of Nazism and the onset of World War II.

These conflicts were fought by loyal, dedicated heroes who seldom understood their underlying reasons or consequences. Each war seems to create the next conflict, i.e., World War II, the "Cold War" with Russia, the "Korean Conflict," Vietnam, Iraq, Afghanistan.

Noting an oft-cited admonition, "Those who ignore history will be bound to repeat it," we seem not to have learned these many lessons of history.

Let us fervently hope for a better way.

Bibliography

Part I 1863, Judson's Civil War Journey

Adams, Blanche V., *The Second Colorado Calvary in the Civil War,* Colorado State Archives.

Brown, Robert Leaman, *Ghost Towns of the Colorado Rockies,* Caldwell, Idaho, Caxton Press, 1968.

Brownlee, Richard S., *Gray Ghost of the Confederacy, Guerrilla Warfare in the West, 1861-1865,* Baton Rouge, Louisiana, Louisiana State University Press, 1958.

Pietkivitch, Alvin J., *Skunk Grove the First Franksville?* Franksville 100 Year Centennial, 1975, Racine, Wisconsin.

Schernekau, August, Potter, James E., Robbins, Edith, *Marching with the First Nebraska, A Civil War Diary,* Norman, Oklahoma, University of Oklahoma Press, 2007.

_____, *Battles of the Civil War,* Map, National Geographic Supplement, April 2005.

_____, *Battle of Chalk Bluff, Rugged and Sublime,* The Civil War in Arkansas, Department of Arkansas Heritage, 1997.

_____, *Civil War in Missouri Facts,* Union Missouri, 1998, The Missouri Commandery of Military Order of the Loyal Legion of the U.S.

_____, *Union Regimental Histories, Colorado, 1st Regiment Cavalry,* The Civil War Archive, A Compendium of the War of Rebellion, Part 3, Weld County Records.

_____, *Visit of the Council to Camp Weld,* Rocky Mountain News, Denver, September 18, 1861.

Part II 1898, Runnie: A Nebraskan in Manila

Hunt, Geoffrey R., *Colorado's Volunteer Infantry in the Philippine Wars, 1898-1899*, Albuquerque, New Mexico, University of New Mexico Press, 2006.

Ingalls, John J., *America's War for Humanity*, New York, N. D. Thompson Publishing Company, 1898.

Linn, Brian McAllister, *The Philippine War 1899-1902*, Lawrence, Kansas, University Press of Kansas, 2000.

Shunk, Capt. F. R., Corps of Engineers, *Map Showing the Operations of Second Division, 8th Army Corps, from March 1st to May 31st 1899*, Library of Congress Division of Maps, ct002452 Manila Vicinity.

Stickney, Joseph L., *Admiral Dewey at Manila and the Complete Story of the Philippines*, Chicago, Illinois, Imperial Publishing Company, 1899.

Thiessen, Thomas D., *The Fighting Nebraska: Nebraska's Imperial Adventure in the Philippines, 1898-1899*, Nebraska History, Fall 1989, Vol.70, No.3, Lincoln, Nebraska, Nebraska State Historical Society, 1989.

Thompson, Lt. Col. R.E., Chief Signal Officer, *Map of Manila and Vicinity Showing Positions of Troops prior to the Battle of February 5th and the Location of Military Telegraph Lines*, Library of Congress Division of Maps, ct002453 Manila and Bay, 1899.

_____, Fremont Tribune, Fremont, Nebraska, August 30, 1899.

Part III 1918, Glenn: A French *Croix de Guerre*

Cope, W. D., *36th Division in World War I*, Texas Military Forces Museum, Austin, Texas.

Palmer, Fredrick, *Our Greatest Battle, The Meuse-Argonne*, New York, Dodd Mead and Company, 1924.

_____, *Historical Sketch 36th Infantry Division*, Texas Military Forces Museum, Austin, Texas.

2d and 36th on Champagne Front, Stars and Stripes, 1918.

America's Greatest Battle III, Third Phase of the Meuse-Argonne, Colliers, Lincoln State Journal, Lincoln, Nebraska, December 8, 1918.

At the Front, Ravenna News, Ravenna, Nebraska, November 29, 1918.

German Staff Chief Makes Reply to Pershing War Story, Lincoln State Journal, Lincoln, Nebraska, May 3, 1931.

Last Battle of the War, World Herald, Omaha, Nebraska, November 17, 1918.

Pershing's Story, Chapter 70, Lincoln State Journal, Lincoln, Nebraska, March 22, 1931.

Twenty Years Ago, American Legion Magazine, Chicago, Illinois, April, May, June, July, August, September, October, November 1938, New York City, New York.

The Thirty-Sixth Division in the Great War, The Arrowhead Divisional Newspaper, A.E.F., Imprinerie, Leon Dauer, Paris, 1919.

About the Author

Eugene Arundel Miller grew up in Lexington, Nebraska, the youngest grandson of Arundel C. Hull, one of the early photographers along the route of the new Transcontinental railroad. Miller's inheritance of Hull's historic photographs led to his research and subsequent publication of *"Railroad 1869, Along the Historic Union Pacific."*

Similarly, the author's inheritance of the family collection of letters sent home by his ancestors in three different wars triggered his research into the history of those eras. His current book, *"Soldiers' Letters Home"* tells those stories

After graduating from Colorado State University and Georgia Institute of Technology, Miller served in the post-Korean War era first as a Navy Seabee, then as a Naval Civil Engineer Corps officer. He lives and has practiced civil and geotechnical engineering in the San Francisco Bay Area for forty-five years. His publications include four previously published historical non-fiction books and articles in various professional journals and magazines.

Book Order Form

TO: Antelope-Press
   410 Monte Vista Ave.
   Mill Valley, CA 94941

SHIP TO: _____

       _____

       _____

       _____

Soldiers' Letters Home _____@ $14.95_____

Railroad 1869   _____@ $29.95   _____

A Traveler's Guide
To Railroad 1869   _____@ $4.95   _____

Photographer of the Early West,
The Story of Arundel Hull_____@ $14.95 _____

Arundel C. Hull, Ghost Photographer
for William H. Jackson ____@ $3.95   _____

                Sub Total   _____

Orders from California only, Tax 9.5 %   _____

   Postage & Handling
   $3.00 first item +
     $ 0.50 each additional item   _____

            TOTAL   _____

(Check or Money Order only please. Sorry, no credit cards.)

CPSIA information can be obtained at www.ICGtesting.com
Printed in the USA
BVOW030717211111

276453BV00006B/6/P